Skiing Fitness

Reach your potential on the slopes

Mark Hines

First published in 2006 by
A&C Black Publishers Ltd
38 Soho Square, London W1D 3
www.acblack.com

ISBN-10 0 713678348
ISBN-13 9780713678345

A CIP catalogue record for this book is available from the British Library.

Typeset in AGaramond by Palimpsest Book Production Ltd.

Note: It is always the responsibility of the individual to assess his or her own fitness capability before participating in any training activity. While every effort has been made to ensure the content of this book is as technically accurate as possible, neither the author nor the publishers can accept responsibility for any injury or loss sustained as a result of the use of this material.

Text and cover design by James Watson
Cover image © Corbis
Images on pages 6, 16 and 130 © Corbis. All the other images © Grant Pritchard

A&C Black uses paper produced with elemental chlorine-free pulp, harvested from managed sustainable forests.

Printed and bound in China

Contents

Acknowledgements

I would like to thank a number of people for making this book possible. Firstly, I would like to thank both of my parents for teaching me to ski from a young age, and for taking me to a number of beautiful places around the world where I could practise.

On a technical level, I would like to thank my dear friend John Hardy, as an authority on all matters relating to biomechanics and exercise prescription. It is through the existence of John that I have always had somebody at hand that I can phone up and argue with about many issues surrounding exercise science and kinesiology. Most importantly, it is good to have somebody to agree with when we find ourselves challenging the status quo.

Also on a technical level, I would like to thank Dr Mike Langran for his input on the sports injuries section. I am most grateful that he allowed me to use some of the statistics and information from his website; www.ski-injury.com

Finally, I would like to thank my two models, Emily and Stephen, for their help in making this book happen. They have both been wonderful colleagues and are good friends. I have enjoyed training with them in the past, and am grateful for the time and commitment that they put in to getting the photographs right for this book.

Introduction

Skiing is becoming more accessible to a greater range of people all over the world. The sport has spread from its origins in Scandinavia to just about anywhere that has a hill and sees some snow. With the growing sophistication of artificial indoor and outdoor slopes, skiing is not only available to more people but can also be practised to a greater standard than on older dry slopes. Despite the growing numbers of practitioners, the increasing number of ski lifts and pistes means that there are many places that can be skied free from the crowds.

With more people skiing on- and off-piste, it is important to ensure that all skiers are appropriately physically conditioned. For those who ski all year round, this can be a good opportunity to improve muscle and joint function, and apply it directly to improve technical skills. For those who go skiing only once or twice a year, being physically conditioned will enable them to get the most pleasure and development from their skiing trips.

The purpose of this book is to introduce you to the most effective exercises for skiing. Indeed, the exercises will develop the body of anyone, regardless of how adept they are at skiing. The plan is to treat the body as a functional unit, developing that unit for the specific tasks required of it when skiing so as to improve technique and fitness. While this is not a book about developing technical skills – something best learned on the slopes – it does set out to train the individual to be better able (from a specific fitness perspective) to develop technical skills.

As an exercise scientist specialising in biomechanics, my work involves studying the way people move and then finding ways to improve their movement and reduce their risk of injury or pain. You may be surprised to learn that there are very few top athletes with fantastic biomechanics. This is not to say that moving badly is good because these people are likely to pick up muscle injuries (we've all heard of footballers and sprinters tearing their hamstrings) and may suffer from even more problems later in life.

Regardless of what level of skier you are – whether an absolute novice or a gold medallist – you can improve your abilities on the slopes and decrease your risk of injury. I have never met anybody who suffered from a *slight* skiing injury, or was only *slightly* sore the day after their first day on the slopes. So, we shall begin at the beginning. We will get you moving properly first, to ensure your joints are doing what they are supposed to, and then we will start increasing the demands of the training over the course of several weeks. This will have the effect of developing the body specifically for the rigours of skiing while maintaining optimal joint positioning. In short, you will be moving properly and performing what I believe to be the best course of skiing programmes ever devised. I write that because most skiing programmes tend to train the legs and arms, which is interesting but not specific enough to do much good, but more on that later.

From a safety perspective, the fitter someone is, the less likely they are to have an accident. There are, however, many types of fitness. Although we tend to have a preconceived idea of what we would describe or recognise as fitness, we can quite easily miss out on some important factors. We could describe a marathon runner as fit, and we could describe an Olympic power-lifter as fit, and although we would be correct both times, they are clearly very different types of fitness, and one type is by no means more important than the other. Someone who plays chess could be described as mentally fit, and they could 'train' to improve their mental fitness, but this in itself would not make them fitter for any physical function.

Flexibility, strength, endurance, power, cardiovascular ability, balance, proprioception (detailed later), stability and nervous function are all important and independent types of fitness. When all these factors that contribute to skiing fitness are developed, physical and mental fatigue can be offset or prevented, thereby improving all-round ability to ski to the best standard that your technique will allow. Technique itself can then be developed far better than if the body lacks sufficient levels of fitness in any of the factors mentioned.

Most importantly, 'fitness', in whatever guise, can be improved through developmental training. This means starting from whatever skiing or exercising background – whether novice, beginner, intermediate, advanced or professional – and improving ability through small but significant steps. The exercises included in this book make up a course of different programmes. They are intended not just to take the beginner to an advanced stage, but to take anybody from any level and allow them the opportunity to make natural and comfortable progressions far beyond those that might be derived from other programmes or by skiing alone.

Skiing is a highly technical sport, and although technical ability can be nurtured through an appropriate exercise programme, actual technical skills are best improved when skiing. What improvements depend upon, however, is the body's ability to recover from bouts of skiing (even down to an individual turn), and react and move accordingly in relation to the skier's speed and the nature of the surface beneath them. Exercise training can be used to prevent fatigue, to ensure muscles have energy for developing power when needed, and to allow the body to react to maintain posture and balance regardless of the demands of the terrain. This can all be brought together to give the skier the supporting tools required to make the most out of their skiing.

Fitness for skiing has to include a number of factors. Most importantly, regardless of the starting point, everybody can benefit from skiing-specific training. The problem is that few people really understand what 'skiing-specific' means, and the abundance of contradictions and misconceptions in the exercise industry could bewilder the most seasoned professional from any background. By the end of this book, however, you should have improved your knowledge of skiing fitness to the point of being an expert on the subject. The goal, therefore, is not only to improve your skiing fitness and ability, but also to increase your understanding of how the body works, and how this relates to what is essentially an original approach to training for one of the oldest sports in the world.

The History of Skiing

As a skier, you are one of more than 200 million skiers in the world today. Not only that, but you are also part of one of the oldest winter traditions. It was around 5000 years ago that people first started strapping skis to their feet. The Norwegians were the first, using skis as they were hunting across the snow-covered Nordic landscape. Skiing then spread across Scandinavia and Russia, initially as a mode of transportation, and eventually as a sport similar to modern cross-country skiing.

Alpine (downhill) skiing was the next stage in the evolution of winter sports. That is not to suggest that cross-country skiing was made redundant, rather that skis were developed that were engineered according to the precise nature of the skiing activity. The first Alpine skiing competition was held in Oslo in the 1850s. A few decades later, skiing spread to the rest of Europe and the United States, where miners entertained themselves with skiing competitions during the winter months. The first slalom was held in Mürren, Switzerland, in 1922, and in 1924 it became the first Olympic Alpine event.

Alpine skiing underwent a huge renaissance in the 1990s with the development of carving skis. There are now more than 70 million snowboarders in the world, with emerging sports such as skiboarding and telemark skiing growing in presence on the slopes. Ski lifts have got faster and increased in number. Together with the expansion and development of ski areas, and improved snow-making facilities, this has allowed the number of winter sports enthusiasts to grow.

People may ski for the challenge, for the sport itself, for the release it brings or simply because it is fun. Whatever the reason, skiing is superb for all-over body strength, particularly for the lower back and legs. It also improves muscular endurance and power, both of which are important as we grow older. Mountain air has health benefits too. It is much less polluted than the air found in cities and has lower oxygen levels. This is why mountain air may cause less free radical damage to the body's cells, which is linked to disease, including cancer.

In addition to the physical benefits, skiing takes the individual to an environment far removed from the stress of everyday life. The contrasts in surroundings offer a monumental release from the mundane, while rekindling and nurturing our desire to explore and master. At the same time, the breathtaking beauty of our natural world may captivate the skier. So, through skiing, we have a medium to escape mental stresses, to improve physical wellbeing and, quite possibly, to reduce our risks of various cancers (providing, of course, that we limit our skin's exposure to direct sunlight).

The Exercise Renaissance

Although exercise training techniques have come a long way, there is still much to be achieved before we can truly believe that we are benefiting our 'health' in a more holistic sense. When it comes to putting a skiing programme into practice, it helps to understand what the options are, because the approach I use is radically different to that used by the majority of the industry. I am not alone in this, and I do not want to be because I would like everybody to get the most out of their investments and their body. But with so few exercise professionals having a platform such as this to promote their ideas to the world, I am rather proud to be one of the first, and hope that this book makes me more friends and comrades than enemies.

Modern exercise training, as we recognise it in health clubs today, came from the strong men of the latter part of the 19th century. The purpose of exercise then was to develop the muscles, which culminated in public displays of strength and muscle size. From those pioneering days, resistance training began evolving into our modern weightlifting, power-lifting and body-building sports and competitions.

Prior to the 1950s, nearly all resistance training involved just dumbbells and barbells. Then, various companies set about manufacturing machines for use by body-builders. The logic was that body-builders could use the machines to train specific muscle groups. These resistance machines also acted as a way of training all the muscles, and became an extra string to the body-builder's bow.

The vast majority of trainers still use exercises and programmes based on body-building techniques from decades ago. Someone may go into a health club with the goal of improving various aspects of their fitness, such as becoming better at sport, losing fat, gaining muscle, improving definition, 'toning up', improving their health, relieving stress, or simply for social reasons. But for almost every goal, the typical trainer will provide an exercise programme based on body-building exercises and techniques.

The problem is that body-building focuses on muscles, and treating the body as a collection of them, whereas in fact the body should be regarded as a unit. If we were to consider the muscles involved in picking something up from a table, the body-building approach would be to consider first the biceps shortening to bend the elbow, thus initiating movement. The movement-based approach of our modern trainers would be more simplistic, because in fact every muscle in the body is going to be involved to some extent in that movement. The body-building logic would ascertain that the best way to improve ability at picking something up from a table is to do biceps exercises. The movement-based expert would advocate simply repeating the exact movement, so that the body is trained as a whole to perform a specific task.

Taking this example one step further, if we wanted to become better at jumping or kicking, the movement-based trainer would advocate repeating the same movement, and might consolidate this by promoting some exercises that improve joint actions for specific parts of that movement. But, regardless of how many exercises are actually chosen, they will all be either very similar or exactly the same as the movement that needs to be produced. A body-building approach, however, might be to take the individual muscles and muscle groups involved in the movement, and then train them individually. This could mean that the person is advised to perform leg extensions, leg presses and leg curls. The problem with this is that we have no confidence in the idea that training in this way will have any carry-over effect whatsoever. What is also important is that training 'muscles' rather than 'movements' may leave the joints untrained and lacking the strength and stability required to prevent injuries.

A large part of this comes down to the body's nervous system. Most of the movements you do every day happen in a very precise manner. When you pick something up, walk, run, sit down, stand up, twist, turn, stick your arm out, close the car door, step up, *everything*, it happens in a certain way. Exercise scientists have analysed the way the body moves. All the muscles in the body are supposed to 'fire' (be activated by nerves) at a certain rate, to a certain degree and in a particular order for every single natural movement. The logic behind 'functional', 'movement-based' exercise training is to embrace this natural way of moving and build on it. Essentially, it involves choosing or creating exercises based on the body's own natural movement patterns.

This means that the body can become stronger and healthier, and better at doing something such as skiing simply by replicating natural movements and adding resistance from the correct direction. If you are using this sort of training, then you are training the body the way that it has developed, and therefore improving joint strength and stability, bone strength, motor control and muscle performance in exactly the way that you want for your goals and for your body.

The danger with the more archaic body-building approach is that this very important aspect of human development and movement is completely disregarded. What is worse is that if you break a movement down into component muscles, and then train them individually, you are teaching the body a different way to activate muscles. This will counter the body's natural movement patterns, and may then have a deleterious effect on the way the body moves and responds to physical stress. Even body-building – the use of resistance training to increase muscle size – can actually be performed using movement-based exercises. If you want to go skiing, then it makes sense to adopt a method of training that embraces this, and sets out to train the body to be better at skiing, rather than just bulking up some of the muscles involved, which then accomplish nothing more than being some extra weight.

Eventually, there will be a fundamental change in the way people design and choose exercises. For now, there are only a few trainers who truly embrace this logic, and here you are offered an insight into its practical application for the improvement of skiing ability.

skiing injuries

A good understanding of skiing injuries is paramount to ensuring that due care is taken to avoid an injury occurring. Such an understanding will not only aid in preparation for skiing, but will also increase awareness on the slopes, and may be of use when choosing ski wear and equipment. Should an injury occur, even when following a thorough preventive programme, then it is important to understand the nature of the injury and how to promote recovery and prevent recurrence. Because the advice given here is general, there is the chance that other individual factors may contribute to an injury, and susceptibility to a specific injury can only be assessed on an individual basis.

This section of the book may have particular appeal to those who have already suffered an injury, or who have friends or relatives who have been injured while skiing. The information aims to improve knowledge of the condition and how it became possible to receive the injury in the first instance.

The overall rate of skiing injuries has halved since initial records in the 1970s. There are a number of reasons for this, including developments in skiing equipment, more attention being paid to fitting the equipment, and general care and safety features on various slopes. In general, the rate of injuries is relatively constant the world over, reflecting improved standards of ski-area management. The biggest reduction in injuries has been to the lower body, which is in relation to the improved safety features of ski boots and release mechanisms. Brakes on skis, which help stop a ski from continuing down the slope following a boot release, have helped to reduce the number of lacerations (cuts) to other skiers.

So, now that I have your attention, it is worth mentioning that there is not *that* much to worry about. Despite the fact that every winter or spring you see someone with a leg cast on, or their hand bandaged, or their arm in a sling, there are actually very few injuries, on average, per skier over the duration of their time skiing. There is always a chance that an injury could happen, however, particularly on the second afternoon of skiing because the person was out of condition, tired, depleted of energy stores, dehydrated, and possibly feeling the after-effects of the first big night of après-ski. The purpose of the rest of this section is to inform you of all the debilitating things that might just happen the next time you strap your skis on, so that we can then look at ways to help prevent that from happening.

One common method for comparing various injuries, and ski injuries overall, is to calculate the mean (average) days between injury (MDBI). This is calculated by dividing the total number of skier days within a season by the number of injuries recorded. The higher the MDBI, the greater the number of days between injuries and the lower the risk. Lower limb injuries occur at a rate of one every 520 days, while upper limb injuries occur once every 1140 days, suggesting that you are twice as likely to injure a lower limb than an upper limb.

The overall MDBI for skiing is approximately 315. This means that an individual has a risk of receiving a skiing injury for every 315 days that they ski. This figure is surprisingly low, and may reflect the fact that many injuries are not recorded, and that treatments are only obtained following return home, if at all. The figure also fails to give an indication of how serious the injuries are, and the likelihood that the skiers will return to the slopes in that or any other skiing season. In short, skiing is a wonderful sport, and to ensure longevity of its enjoyment, it is necessary to take steps to prevent injuries from occurring.

Falls are a common cause of injury, accounting for between 75 and 85 per cent of skiing injuries. The majority of injuries caused by falls are sprains, followed by fractures, lacerations and dislocations.

Because of the injury risk of falls, skiers tend to fight incredibly hard to maintain balance when they find themselves out of control. However, this is likely to lead to an increase in speed, difficulty in regaining balance and control, and risk of receiving a serious injury. Hence, many ski instructors will recommend that a skier attempts to encourage a fall when struggling to maintain or regain balance. The intention is to fall under reasonable control and at a reasonable speed, rather than risk falling shortly afterwards anyway, but in a much less controlled and more dangerous position.

As a skier falls, the head should be tucked in, preferably with the skis close together and parallel, with the arms at the side. The fall should be off to the side rather than over the back of the skis, and care should be taken to release the poles, to prevent an injury from either falling on them or having the straps damage the thumb. An injury is most likely to occur from sprawling the arms and legs and hitting the snow haphazardly. Although a perfect fall – when an immediate recovery is not possible – is rarely a possibility, it is far better to bail out early rather than increase the risk of serious injury by falling with no control whatsoever.

Connective Tissue

Connective tissue is the most abundant and varied tissue in the body. It includes bone, cartilage, skin and even blood and components of the immune system. Connective tissue is important for attachments of muscle to bone, bone to bone, and muscle to muscle. Here, we are interested in breaks in the skin (lacerations), breaks in bones (fractures) and damage to the connective surfaces around muscles, bones and joints (strains, sprains and dislocations). Sprains and strains are among the most common connective tissue injuries in all sports.

A sprain is a stretch, partial tear or complete tear of a ligament (ligaments are fibrous bands of connective tissue that bind one bone to another). The purpose of a ligament is to stabilise a joint and prevent excessive movement. Ligaments are relatively inelastic, meaning that a strong force that moves a joint beyond its natural range of movement can lead to damage. Ligaments also generally lack the blood supply of muscles and many other connective tissues, meaning that they can take a long time to heal.

The body is made up of three types of muscle tissue:

1. **Cardiac muscle** is the muscle of the heart.
2. **Smooth muscle** is located in some internal organs, including parts of the digestive system, where it is involved in helping food move along the gut.
3. **Skeletal muscle** is the muscle we see that gives our body shape, that allows us to move our joints and to perform movements and exercise (accepting that the heart obviously plays a vital supporting role as well).

In fact, all three types of muscle work in synergy to allow us to perform movements, to breathe and to live. With regard to injury, we are most interested in skeletal muscle tissue. A strain is an injury to the skeletal muscle tissue, caused by overstretching, overexertion or a direct trauma. In some cases, areas of skeletal muscle tissue can be completely severed from surrounding muscle fibres or tendons (tendons are the connective tissues that bind muscle to bone).

A dislocation (or 'luxation') occurs when connective tissues around a joint surface are damaged, allowing the joint surfaces to separate. This can be the result of a pulling or twisting movement to the joint itself, causing the bone surfaces to stretch and then tear the supporting connective tissues completely. A 'subluxation' occurs when the connective tissues are stretched to the point of causing damage, but are not completely torn.

Bones have a number of functions, including production of red blood cells, attachments for muscles, levers for movement and protection of internal organs. A fracture occurs when sufficient force is placed on a bone to cause it to break. There are various types of fracture, and can be caused by a single force acting directly towards the bone from one end or across the bone (as used to occur frequently to the shin bone before binding release mechanisms were improved). Fractures can also be caused by excessive twisting forces on a particular bone, as can be generated during falls. Because some bones are also important for protection, such as the skull and the ribcage, it is clear that significant collision forces to these areas can result in fractures. If such injuries do occur, then it is possible that the associated internal organs were also affected, so swift medical attention is vital.

Upper Body Injuries

There has been little change in the reported rates of head, shoulder and thumb injuries since the 1970s. Injuries to the upper extremities account for approximately 30–40 per cent of all skiing injuries. The four main injuries to Alpine skiers are dislocated shoulders, fractured clavicle (collarbone), fractured humerus (upper arm bone) and AC joint subluxations (the AC joint joins the collarbone to the top of the shoulder joint).

Head Injuries

The types of head injuries seen in Alpine skiers vary from minor bumps and lacerations to far more serious, life-threatening fractures. Most injuries, however, are minor and can be administered to quite simply. Although a range of injuries can occur due to the same cause, such as collision with another object, it is often the speed of impact that predicts severity of injury.

Most ski-related deaths involve trauma to the head. These are often due to a high-speed collision with a tree, pylon, rock or other slope user. At lesser speeds, an injury to the same area of the head may lead to a slight concussion, but even this will mean foregoing some time on the slopes. Even minor head injuries can lead to headaches, light-headedness and nausea, and poor concentration. These lesser injuries still need to be taken seriously, and should be assessed by a doctor as soon as possible, and definitely before returning to the slopes or driving. If someone receives a head injury that causes a lack of consciousness, then they need to be taken to a hospital for assessment and observation. Injuries to children should be taken very seriously, and any perceived threshold for when to seek medical advice for an adult should be significantly lowered for children.

Spinal Injuries

Spinal injuries themselves are fortunately rare, but the mechanisms by which they can be initiated are far more common. This means that it is best to be safe if someone has fallen and there is the possibility that they damaged their spine in the process.

There are two parts of the spine. The first is the bony apparatus that makes up the vertebral column. The vertebrae, like other bones, act as levers to allow movement to occur. Although the movements of individual segments of the spine are relatively small, when acting together much greater movements and ranges of motion are possible. Because the spine is so mobile as a total unit, any excessive movements, such as twisting or bending, or combinations of movements can lead to strains of the muscles that attach to the vertebrae. This can be very painful, and because the muscles are always being used in normal movement, they can often take a long time to heal as they rarely receive sufficient rest. The purpose of the exercises in this book is essentially to strengthen these muscles and train the necessary movements to help prevent just these types of injuries from occurring. Although an injury to these muscles may be incredibly painful, the problem is essentially no more than a muscle strain.

The other function of the vertebrae is to protect the spinal cord. The spinal cord is the nerve highway to and from the brain, with all the major nerve roads running from it all the way down to its base. The higher up the spinal cord, the greater the importance of the area. For example, a tear in the spinal cord towards its base may be disabling, but there are lots of possibilities for rehabilitation and protection of quality of life. Higher up towards the brain, however, tears may be permanently disabling, including total paralysis, and with less likelihood of rehabilitation. Injuries to the spinal cord can happen when such extreme movements of the spinal column occur that shearing forces directly damage nerves or the spinal cord itself. Severe impacts and other trauma can cause a similar effect.

Any of these injuries, whether to skeletal muscle that attaches to the spinal column or shearing forces to the spinal cord, will be caused by excessive movements of the spine. These excessive forces, most likely involving many different movements and angular forces, may be caused by particularly bad falls, jumps with poor landings and avalanches. Although the likelihood of a spinal cord injury is low, it is essential to avoid moving the casualty unless their life is in immediate danger, and to send someone to get help from the ski patrol.

Shoulder Injuries

The shoulder joint is complex and consists of the upper arm bone (humerus), collarbone (clavicle) and shoulder blade (scapula). The clavicle, in turn, joins to the acromium (at the top outside end of the scapula) at one end and the sternum (breastbone) at the other. The muscle attachments for these bones extend across the chest, the back and the arms. There is also other connective tissue, such as tendons, ligaments and cartilage, which can all be damaged through skiing-related injuries.

Dislocation of the shoulder can occur when the arm is outstretched, and there is sufficient force acting in the opposite direction to that in which the skier's momentum is travelling. This could be an upward and/or backward force during a fall. It could also occur when the skier is moving too fast or out of control and grasps a fence, tree, planted ski pole, or uses another skier as an anchor, to help stop.

Once a dislocation has occurred, there is an 85 per cent chance of dislocating the same joint in the future, due to weaknesses in the connective tissue. This supports the reason for strengthening joints through resistance exercise prior to skiing, and for adhering to physiotherapy advice for effective rehabilitation. In some cases, when the shoulder joint is repeatedly dislocated, with comparatively minor trauma causing the injury, surgery may be required to stabilise the joint and help prevent further dislocations from occurring.

Dislocations and subluxations can also occur to the ligament that binds the acromium to the clavicle (the AC joint). This dislocation, or subluxation, can result from a direct impact to the outside of the humerus. A dislocation to this joint is very rare, with subluxations being more common, and surgery is required in only a few cases to bring the acromium and clavicle closer together again. It is also possible to fracture the clavicle directly; this is often the result of an impact that radiates upwards from the humerus.

Injuries to the Humerus

Fractures to the upper arm bone can result from a direct blow, such as during a collision, or falling onto an outstretched hand. The fractures can occur either across the shaft of the bone or to the end of the bone next to the shoulder joint.

Skier's Thumb

Skier's thumb is the name for an injury to the joint where the base of the thumb joins the bones of the hand, affecting one of the ligaments that joins the bones together. Injury to this ulnar collateral ligament (UCL) of the thumb is the most common upper limb injury for skiers. An injury to this ligament is second only to a medial collateral ligament (MCL) injury in the knee in terms of frequency of occurrence in skiers. Injury to the UCL tends to occur when a skier falls onto an outstretched hand while still gripping the ski pole. The movement causes the thumb to be pulled outwards, leading to injury of the joint.

Many people underestimate the significance of a hand injury. Because big, whole body movements are still possible, it is easy to neglect proper treatment for a thumb injury. The scale of the problem may become obvious only when it is sufficiently awkward and painful to perform everyday tasks, such as writing or typing, eating, carrying bags, drinking tea, using a television remote control, and dressing and undressing. In short, injuries to the thumb are serious, and proper care should be taken to treat the injury if it occurs, and to maximise opportunities for proper rehabilitation. Failure to do so may result in long-term disability.

Injury to the UCL can be reduced by using the straps as well as holding on to the pole, instead of holding the pole directly. The hand should be placed upwards through the underside of the strap before holding the pole. This increases the likelihood that the hand will release the pole during a fall. The goal is to ensure that the pole is let go of completely during a fall. Ideally, if no straps were used and the pole was released during a fall, then the pole would end up further away and the risk of injury would be reduced. Unfortunately, it is more likely, from a psychological viewpoint at least, that a skier will try to keep the pole as close as possible during a fall, if for no other reason than to save themselves a walk afterwards. Of course, if the UCL is damaged, then skiing with a pole in the hand is not a possibility anyway!

If skiing in deep powder, the poles are more important, so using the straps is even more valid. New devices are being developed that involve clipping the poles directly to the glove, or securing the hand to the pole in some other manner. At the moment there are too few users to measure the effectiveness of these tools, and the key thing to remember in any case is simply to ensure that the poles are released during a fall. If you can master not using the straps and still releasing the poles, then you will be even less likely to suffer skier's thumb.

Lower Body Injuries

When most people think of skiing injuries, they tend to think about injuries to the knees and legs. Fractures of the lower leg bones (tibia and fibula) used to be common before binding release mechanisms were improved, although it is still vitally important to ensure that bindings are fitted correctly. Fractures to the top of the shinbone (tibial plateau) account for approximately 1 per cent of all skiing injuries, and tend to occur following a bad landing after a jump, which transmits huge compressive forces to that area of bone.

Some fractures still occur to the shinbones when the body is forced forwards of the ski boots, and it is essential to check all equipment for proper releasing before use. Even so, these fractures can still occur if the skis plough into deep, soft snow, and the body's momentum continues forwards as the skis come to a stop.

Cartilage injuries are also quite common in skiers. In particular, the menisci that sit on top of the tibial plateau can be damaged during a harsh twisting movement of the knee, when the knee is bent, and is usually accompanied by other injuries to the area. Injuries to the meniscus itself occur in approximately 5–10 per cent of all ski injuries.

The evolution of binding release mechanisms has not, however, accomplished very much in the prevention of knee injuries. Damage to the knee ligaments accounts for about a third of all ski injuries. Such injuries can be slow to rehabilitate, although it can happen with good physiotherapy and appropriate exercise, and in some cases the injury might be bad enough to prevent the individual from ever being able to ski again.

Knee Injuries

Few people appreciate the complexity of the knee joint until they injure it. The knee is able to bend and straighten, and also has a small amount of rotational movement available when bent. The joint is where the tibia of the lower leg meets the femur of the upper leg, with the patella (kneecap) to the front. The ends of the bones are covered in cartilage, including the thick menisci at the top of the tibia, into which the femur sits. The bones are joined together by a number of ligaments. These include medial collateral and lateral collateral ligaments on the inside and outside of the knee respectively, and anterior and posterior cruciate ligaments coming into the knee and on to the tibia from the femur. Because the role of the ligaments is to stabilise the knee and keep the bones in the correct positions, injury to these ligaments is a common result of a bad landing.

Skiing injuries to the knee will often involve the medial collateral ligament (MCL), anterior cruciate ligament (ACL) or the meniscus, or a combination of the three. A key purpose of this book is to strengthen and develop the connective tissue of the various joints of the body to help prevent injury. If the knee has been injured, then it is even more important to engage in an appropriate exercise programme to help guard against recurrence. A physiotherapist should be able to assess any inherent weaknesses, imbalances or susceptibility to injury, which can then lead to individual advice regarding the exercise programmes.

Any obvious deformity of the knee, accompanied by local tenderness, swelling and the inability to either straighten the leg fully or to bear weight on it, would suggest a serious knee injury. There may also be an audible popping sound when the injury occurs. Any of these signs would suggest a requirement for medical attention as soon as possible, and definitely avoidance of the slopes until the knee has been thoroughly assessed and an accurate evaluation given. Because it is possible to function with various degrees of ligament sprain – even complete tears (or 'ruptures') – it is particularly important to have injuries checked to prevent further damage.

A damaged ligament will limit mobility and joint range of motion. Because most ligaments do not have a good blood supply, they can take significantly longer to heal than some other connective tissue injuries. This may mean that the knee collapses during activity, and extra care should be taken to ensure that the approach to therapy and exercise is kept steady and progressive. Reconstructive surgery may sometimes be required to bring parts of the ruptured ligament back together. Full rehabilitation may sometimes take a year, making it all the more important to ensure that skiing preparation focuses on developing areas that were previously damaged (something many people instinctively want to avoid).

MCL Injuries

Medial collateral ligament (MCL) damage is the most common injury in Alpine skiing. This ligament stabilises the knee in side-to-side movements. A slow twisting fall, or the prolonged maintenance of the snowplough position where the tibia is twisted outwards in relation to the femur, can cause sprains to this ligament. A higher speed twisting movement, such as from 'catching an edge' with one lower leg twisting outwards quickly, can also sprain the MCL.

The snowplough is the technique commonly adopted by beginners, with a wide stance and the legs pointed inwards. This position makes it difficult to transmit muscular forces down the legs effectively, and one or both legs can easily be made unstable. Conversely, a parallel stance, with the skis not too close together, is more stable but allows greater speeds to be achieved. While this is clearly a good theoretical basis for avoiding MCL injuries, the greater speeds do increase the likelihood of a more serious injury from a fall. Lying between the snowplough and parallel skiing is the 'stem-turn', a technique utilised by intermediates before progressing to full parallel skiing. Here, one ski is kept straight and the other is pushed out into a 'half-snowplough' position. The problem with the stem-turn is that it does not permit the same control at speed as parallel skiing does, so can lead to injuries in skiers who are attempting slopes too advanced for their technique.

The key to prevention of MCL injuries is due care and personal responsibility when skiing. When choosing ski runs it is important to ensure that you can be challenged and try new techniques without the risk of being out of control and unable to stop or turn efficiently. Proper preparation and conditioning is paramount to maximising your enjoyment of the slopes.

ACL Injuries

Prior to the millennium, anterior cruciate ligament (ACL) injuries occurred at a rate of about 2200 MDBI, and this figure had been static for quite some time. Since then the figure has started to reduce, due to the development of carving skis (*see* below). The rate of knee sprains, particularly sprains to the ACL, is not related to ski bindings. This is largely due to the fact that ski bindings are designed to release due to excess forces at the foot and shin, and they cannot detect direct forces at the knee. Hence, although we have seen a decrease in fractures to the tibia and fibula, the rate of injuries to the knee has changed relatively little.

In most cases, it is the tail of the ski that is involved in causing the ACL injury. In normal movement, the heel acts as a short pivot for the leg over the foot. When wearing skis, however, the 'heel' of the foot is effectively displaced quite some way behind the ankle. This then acts as a 'phantom foot', and when balance is lost backwards, that phantom foot creates a greater distance over which to fall backwards. This action leads to an overstretching of the knee, and the ACL is often sprained in the process. Significant shearing forces can also sprain the ACL, such as during a high-speed twisting fall or 'catching an edge'. Rehabilitation of these injuries can be quite difficult, and in some cases will require surgery to bring the two ends of the ligament closer together (for significant partial or complete ligament ruptures).

ACL injuries are now being reduced through the development of new carving skis, which are shorter overall and have a shorter area behind the ski boot. The reduction in ACL injuries has been observed since carving skis first became popular in the year 2000. It is possible that decreasing the required forces for binding release could prevent *some* ACL injuries, although this may lead to skis being released from relatively minor knocks. This is currently being experimented with in France, where reports suggest a reduction in total ACL injuries (the lower ACL injuries could also just be the effect of more people using the shorter carving skis).

Another mechanism for inducing an ACL injury is directly through the boot. This can occur when a skier loses balance to the rear when attempting a jump. If the legs straighten, then the skier will likely land on the tails of the skis, which then causes the back of the ski boot to push against the back of the calf muscles. This pushes the tibia forwards of the femur and sprains or ruptures the ACL. A similar path of force, separating the tibia and femur, can occur when an upright and usually stationary skier is hit in the lower leg from the side or behind by a falling slope user (often a snowboarder). Other means of causing damage to the ACL include twisting falls or when skiing the moguls.

DOMS

Delayed-onset muscle soreness (DOMS) is the uncomfortable feeling that often occurs when we begin a new exercise programme, or push our body more than it is used to. DOMS is an indication that the body has been pushed hard and that the affected muscles require time to recover. The cause of the sore feeling is poorly understood. For some time, many people thought that the soreness was related to lactic acid in the muscles, but this is removed and recycled soon after stopping exercise, with most of it removed within half an hour of completing the session.

What is important to understand is that if muscle fibres require recovery, then this will have an effect on skiing performance. In short, using muscles that have not recovered means the body will under-perform, and this may lead to premature fatigue and an increased risk of injury. Limiting muscle soreness is a combination of eating the correct nutrients, and building up steadily through an exercise training programme, rather than launching in too fast and working significantly harder than the body is used to. The intention is that the progressive nature of the exercise programmes in this book will help prepare the muscles for skiing, and so reduce the likelihood, severity and/or duration of DOMS after a day of skiing.

Stretching has also been hypothesised to prevent muscle soreness. This is unlikely, but the wringing action that stretching has on the muscle fibres may help to remove some toxins and any damaged components of cells, and therefore speed recovery. This idea is highly speculative, however, and there is no strong, tested evidence that this is the case. But as it does not hurt, then it is certainly worth performing a few stretches at the end of a day's skiing.

Collisions

Collisions on the slopes are a common cause of injury. Some people assume that the ski slope is their personal playground, and forget that it is a public thoroughfare with rules and regulations. Collisions may happen when an inexperienced skier loses control as they ski over some ice, or else if someone is skiing at such a speed that they cannot avoid other skiers or obstacles in their path. On some slopes, where routes go through areas of woodland, there is an increased risk of colliding with trees or other skiers on the same tracks.

Collisions with obstacles account for 90 per cent of all skiing fatalities. Trees are the most common cause of these fatalities (60 per cent). Collisions with other people account for approximately 10 per cent of all fatalities. There is debate as to how much the wearing of helmets might protect against fatalities. While helmets may protect against many head injuries, including some lacerations, bruises and fractures, they cannot protect against forces to the base of the skull and neck, which lead to many of the most severe injuries. The best means of protecting against collisions will always be to remain vigilant and aware of other slope users, and never to allow yourself to ski too fast for your own skills and technique to control.

Minimising Risks

Aside from the importance of an appropriate training programme, and proper rehabilitation from injury before skiing again, there are a number of other important factors for preventing injuries when going to the slopes. The binding of each ski should be checked every day before skiing. The bindings need to be adjusted according to height and weight, as well as for the size of the boot itself. Clothing should obviously be warm, but it should not be too loose, otherwise it could catch on ski lifts, branches, fences or other skiers.

At the start of each day, it is important to go down an easy slope, both to warm up and to get an idea of snow conditions. When skiing, always be alert for ice patches, rocks and areas of powder. In particular, try to pay attention to other skiers, and notice if they have difficulty over certain areas where nothing is obviously difficult. Any particularly challenging slopes or jumps that you might have been eyeing up the night before should be attempted earlier on in the day. By the afternoon, fatigue will probably be setting in, so it is important to take it easier then to avoid the risk of causing an accident.

Even on popular slopes it is important to ski with a partner; someone who can help immediately if there is a problem. When skiing off-piste, at least one partner – preferably three or four – is essential. Make sure you both know the route down the mountain (more so for off-piste), and the person lower down the slope should always stop and wait if they lose sight of their partner above them.

Conditioning for Injury Prevention

If an exercise programme includes floor-based work for the abdominals and other core muscles, then I can only hope that these are supposed to be functional exercises for the skier once they have fallen over. They are certainly little use to the skier while they are – as nature intended the skier to be – upright. Likewise, unless you have a really fancy contraption that allows you to ski in some sort of machine, then machine exercises are also somewhat pointless. The only way to *train* the body to be better at skiing, rather than exercising muscles almost for the sake of it, is to train the body in *precisely the same way* as it needs to be utilised.

If you are skiing then you are going to be leaning forwards, squatting, transferring weight from one leg to another and at the same time rotating the torso and pushing down on a pole; and that is *precisely* what you should be doing in training. Even more specifically, the depth of that squat and the power generated will depend upon the skier's level of ability, the speed at which they are travelling, the steepness of the slope, the depth and hardness of the snow, and the angle of the turn. All of this needs to be not just *replicated* but, wherever possible, *duplicated* in training. It is all very well becoming fitter and better conditioned for lifting weights in a gym and pedalling a bicycle, but if the goal is to become fitter and better conditioned for skiing, then most books on training can be thrown clear of the window.

This philosophy is not simply to make people better and more proficient skiers; it is also to strengthen and protect the body against the very injuries referred to in this section. As we have seen, the spine, the shoulder and the knee are all susceptible to serious and debilitating injuries, and while there can be no guarantee of prevention in everyone, any steps taken to reduce the risk of injury will allow for greater enjoyment and confidence on the slopes. Awareness of the mechanisms of injury should also alert the skier to possibly dangerous positions, which can then be averted, thereby offering a direct means of injury prevention when on the slopes.

Flexibility for Injury Prevention

Appropriate levels of flexibility are required to ensure that the skier has functional control of the limbs, even when they are thrown in extended positions. If, for example, the skier has a leg knocked out to one side due to an obstacle, some ice or a bad turn, the greater their flexibility then the further that leg can move away from the body before an injury occurs. Not only that, but there will also be a greater range of movement within which the skier can control that leg and bring it back into a normal position. When skiing, these things happen at speed, so it is important to train the body to move through appropriate ranges of motion at speed.

Food and Drink

Hydration is important for maintaining proper brain function and coordination. Even 1 per cent dehydration can have a negative effect on performance. Because of the amount of clothing worn, and how absorbent it is, it is often difficult to be aware of how much you are sweating when you ski. This is also true of exposed skin, as the effects of wind and moving through the dry air often whip sweat away, so it is difficult to know that you are becoming dehydrated. The thirst mechanism is also very inefficient, as by the time you are thirsty you are already dehydrated, and only a small amount of water will quench thirst but not significantly improve hydration status. Alcohol and caffeine have a diuretic effect, causing fluids to be taken from the body, and increasing the risk of dehydration. Any suggestion that alcohol is just what the doctor ordered for anyone stranded on a mountain is pure myth.

Food is also important, and often overlooked, as people want to maximise their time on the slopes. The body requires energy from carbohydrate and fat stores, and carbohydrate is depleted very easily. Carbohydrate is stored in the liver and muscles, and a small amount is always in the blood to supply the brain and nervous system. *Glucose is the only fuel for the brain!* This means that if there is no glucose, the brain is starved of energy, and there will be a significant effect on coordination, judgement and performance. The carbohydrates stored in the muscles cannot be used by the rest of the body, and what is in the liver is depleted by keeping the brain active during the night. This means that a good breakfast will contain plenty of carbohydrates, and carbohydrate levels should then be topped up during the course of the day. Fats and proteins are also important, and as a fuel they allow for a slow release of energy, meaning that they will be better for keeping the body fuelled during the day.

Skiing is exercise performed across a number of hours, and this needs to be reflected in how much is eaten. Stored carbohydrate levels need to be topped up after a day's skiing to ensure there will not be a day-to-day negative trend in the amount of energy available. An energy deficit can be compensated for by eating anything, not just carbohydrates, as the body will naturally convert what it can and store it as energy. A lack of energy *will* increase the likelihood of injury, and must be guarded against.

Temperature

The temperature on pistes can change very quickly, and this makes it difficult to have one set of clothes that will be suitable for the whole day. This is not helped by the fact that mountains can throw up their own weather systems very quickly. Combine this with areas of exposure and areas of shadow, together with changing body temperatures depending on how much effort is going into skiing, and there are possibilities for dangerous temperature fluctuations in either direction.

The answer is to wear layered clothing, so that layers can be added and removed as necessary. It does mean carrying a bag – at least one in a group – but this should be the case anyway for carrying water and some food. Clothing should also include a good hat and something to cover the mouth.

The effects of extremes of temperature are difficult to notice. If you feel negatively affected by the temperature in any way, either in the form of shivering or an unusual feel to the skin, then it is time to assess clothing and find a solution. Exposure to the cold can lead to frostbite, caused when cells in the extremities of the hands and feet, and the face, become frozen. Frostbite will cause a number of symptoms, including pain and a burning sensation, tingling and numbness. The skin may turn hard and white, peeling off or becoming blistered and then discoloured. Sufferers of frostbite should be taken somewhere warm and dry, and any restrictive clothing should be loosened or removed to aid circulation to the area. Medical assistance should be sought early to help prevent permanent damage.

Hypothermia, where the body has become too cold, is the result of being kept too long in a cold environment. Symptoms of hypothermia include goose bumps and shivering, numbness, confusion, difficultly speaking, stumbling and feelings of depression. The further into hypothermia a person drifts, the more pronounced their symptoms. Shivering will become worse, as will coordination and sight. Eventually, if the symptoms remain unchecked, the person may become unconscious and die. The most important thing to remember is that someone suffering from extremes of heat or cold will be unlikely to be as aware of their symptoms as someone watching them closely. Even if the individual is aware that they have a problem, they are likely to go into denial, which means that someone needs to be assertive in ensuring that they are taken to safety as soon as possible (not the scenic route).

Someone suffering from hypothermia can be warmed in the initial stages by putting on more clothing and being taken somewhere warm and dry. The further into hypothermia someone goes, the less able the body is to warm itself, and so the body heat of another individual can help to restore some warmth.

Children lack the ability to be aware of their temperature in the same way that adults are. This means that extra care and attention should be paid to supervising children on the slopes. Regular breaks for rehydration are more important, and any complaints regarding the temperature should be taken even more seriously than from an adult.

Prevention of cold illnesses is far more important than cures. As well as proper clothing, it is necessary to ensure good hydration, to eat well and to avoid alcohol and certain medications, which may affect the body's ability to maintain its correct temperature, as well as possibly leading to drowsiness. If you have been prescribed medication, then it is advisable to check with your GP before using it during exercise.

Most important is to get anyone suffering from the effects of cold off the slopes and somewhere warm and dry. If someone is getting overheated then layers come off, fluids go in, and you stop exercising until you feel completely back to normal.

Summary

Accidents from skiing can lead to injury in just about any part of the body. In this section, particular attention has been paid to the common injuries to the upper and lower body. Avoidance of injury is the key, and this should take place in various stages. Initially, avoidance is down to proper preparation with conditioning training and an assessment from a physiotherapist. When preparing to go out on the slopes, it is necessary to dress appropriately, and ensure that a good breakfast is eaten before leaving to spend the day skiing.

When on the slopes, breaks should be taken regularly to rehydrate and eat. Alcohol should be avoided when skiing and kept to a minimum in the après-ski.

Avoid accidents on the slopes by being aware of what other slope users are doing, and especially if they are having difficulties over particular areas of the slope. Also, beware of the dreaded children's ski schools, where the teacher is leading a snake of children down the slope, with every child hanging on to the poles of the child in front. This is often worse when the slope changes from an advanced slope at the top to a lower intermediates' or beginners' slope at the bottom. Hence, there are advanced skiers coming down the slope at speed, and then a bottleneck occurs as the snake of children cuts off one half of the slope, and everybody else is trying to squeeze a turn in at the same time on the same part of the slope.

If a fall does occur, try to limit damage by letting go of the poles and keeping the arms tucked in to the body, and aim to fall over to one side rather than off the back of the skis. Try to avoid sitting down on the tail of the skis as this can increase the risk of an ACL injury. Avoid straightening the legs or arms, and do not try to break the landing by sticking a hand out towards the slope. Once the fall has happened, come to a complete stop, get the skis perpendicular to the slope (or cross them) and get up. Do not try to get up while still sliding as this may lead to further damage, especially around the knee joint. Injuries can happen during recovery attempts once control has been lost at the beginning of a fall. Falling gracefully early is better than either falling badly later on or regaining balance and spraining the knee.

Do not attempt a jump unless you have been given sound advice by an instructor. Also, ensure that if you are going to start jumping, that you do it earlier in the day after a warm-up, and that you begin on easier jumps rather than the more impressive ones. Check the area of the landing first by skiing over it (provided no-one is preparing for a jump at the time). Check for deep snow or powder, ice and rocks, and whether a turn is needed shortly after landing. When landing, it is important to land evenly on both skis, with the knees bent and leaning slightly forwards.

If injured, it is best to avoid skiing until completely rehabilitated. This is not just to prevent further injury to yourself, but also to protect other skiers who might be involved in an accident with you if you are unable to use your normal level of control and skill.

If going off-piste, then proper preparation will include taking maps, a compass and food and water. Emergency transmitters are also important to have on the person for use if caught in an avalanche. If tired, take a break and wind down. Have something to eat and drink, and if you still feel tired call it a day. Most injuries occur when the skier is tired, so it is best not to risk injuring yourself and others, and make a start on the après-ski instead.

Bibliography

www.ski-injury.com/intro.htm
www.ski-injury.com/nordic.htm
www.ski-injury.com/alpine.htm
www.ski-injury.com/knee.htm
www.orthoinfo.aaos.org/
www.olympic.org/
www.iasm.com/brochure.html
www.sportsmedicine.about.com/
www.healthlink.mcw.edu/article/975515965.html
www.sportsinjurybulletin.com/archive/skiers-injuries.html

the exercise programmes

The Background

Exercise, like dieting, is an industry. Exercise itself could be free, without the need for any equipment. However, in order to utilise the various methods of training required for an all-encompassing programme, it may be necessary to buy a few specific pieces of equipment. Exercise, fundamentally, should be about health and improving people's way of life. Likewise, information on diets should be about health and healthy eating, even if that is with a particular goal in mind. It seems a shame, therefore, that both industries have become so commercialised. This means that companies will jump on anything that looks profitable, with no particular interest in whether or not it will do any good, or even if it will do any long-term harm.

The exercise equipment featured in this book is used because of its relevance to functional training for skiing. Maybe in a few years another piece of equipment will come out that is an improvement on what I have used here, but it might offer only a fractional benefit. Fads and trends will come and go, and I want to use equipment that has a real purpose. So feel free not to spend a million pounds on the next 'functional skiing machine' because it is probably flawed. The basics are best; just good old-fashioned medicine balls and an unstable surface.

You need to do a number of different types of exercise to improve skiing performance and reduce the risk of injury. While resistance training is important for developing the muscles to exert power and also for transitions through various postures and techniques, cardiovascular fitness is required to prevent fatigue (among other things), and flexibility training (stretching) is needed to allow the body to maintain optimal postures. In addition, balance and proprioceptive training is required to improve technique and reduce the risk of falls.

While flexibility and cardiovascular training are quite straightforward ('work a bit harder than you did last time and keep improving'), the balance, proprioception and resistance training components all require a much more detailed approach. For this reason, a number of progressive programmes have been designed to take someone – regardless of exercise experience – through all the phases necessary to develop excellent skiing potential. Much can be learned on the slopes, but a couple of weeks of skiing is not enough time for the body to make all the adaptations necessary to turn a beginner into a competent advanced skier. Although proper technique can only really be learned and perfected when skiing, the muscles, nervous system, heart and lungs can all be prepared in advance.

The resistance training exercises are designed specifically for skiing. These exercises also have a number of beneficial side-effects, such as toning and strengthening the muscles, improving bone mineral density (a measure of bone health), improving heart and lung function, and reducing body fat (if maintaining the same diet). The cardiovascular exercises will complement these benefits, as well as helping to reduce blood pressure and cholesterol levels, and improving mental alertness. The key is not to do too much, and if you feel tired regardless of how much sleep you have, then it might be time to reduce the number of days exercising. The resistance training can be performed a couple of days a week, as can the cardiovascular exercises, but this can then be tailored according to the individual (resistance training more than three times a week is not advisable). From a practical point of view, it is often most convenient to perform cardiovascular exercise at the end of the resistance training session.

A specific approach to ski training is required, as we have seen (*see*

'The Exercise Renaissance', page 11). Training the legs by doing leg presses, for example, will only improve the body's ability to perform leg presses, not to ski. Much thought, practice and discussion have gone into ensuring that the exercises included in this book are of great practical relevance. Because there are few effective skiing exercises available, most of the exercises in this book are hybrids of relatively common functional exercises, which have been adapted to make them highly specific to skiing. This being the case, it is unlikely that anybody will recognise many of the exercises from experience, so close attention needs to be paid to the photographs and instructions.

Throughout the entire resistance training section, there is only one floor-based exercise. This is because that exercise is very useful for training for recovery from falls on the slopes. With that one exception, there is no point in training the body when on the floor in a skiing-specific programme. The most effective skiing tends to be exhibited when upright on the skis, so that is how the exercises should be. From that basic principle, everything reflects the precise positions and movements of skiing. This makes the exercise programmes absolutely superb for improving Alpine skiing performance. They may be of some use for Nordic skiing and snowboarding, but this book is intended purely for Alpine skiers.

Although a lot of information regarding technique can be understood by looking at the photographs of the exercises and the text accompanying them, personal skiing experience will also be a huge benefit. If you ski in a particular way, try to reflect those postures during the exercises that look similar. Watching skiing on the television, especially slalom competitions, will also give a useful idea as to how the exercises are supposed to be performed.

The speed at which the exercises are carried out should also be based on experience, if possible. To begin with, all the exercises should be performed in a reasonably slow and steady manner so that the position of the joints can be monitored and corrected accordingly. Over the weeks of each programme, that initial speed can be improved upon to bring it more into line with the speeds of movement experienced when skiing. The point of the specific programme is not just to teach the muscles to move a certain way, or to make them more efficient at doing so, but it is also to make the muscles move at the speeds that will be required of them when actually skiing. Starting slowly is essential for perfecting technique, and a slow start should always be adopted during the initial warm-up set. Once competent in the movements, then it is time to start working at a faster pace. Control is still most important, but appropriate speed comes in at a close second. The point is not to teach the body to be slow.

Training Cycles

The first time you use this programme it should, ideally, be commenced nine months prior to skiing. This is a 'perfect world' scenario, which ensures very high competence in all of the areas required to suit the goals of this book. Accepting that few of us live in a perfect world where we can dedicate this much time to skiing, the whole process has been put into three different training cycles:

1. The perfect world cycle, where the programme is spread out over nine months
2. An abbreviated course, which fits into about three months of training
3. A cycle intended for the second year of training onwards – an example of how someone could train over the course of a year to ensure they are at optimal fitness for skiing.

How these cycles actually fit around other responsibilities and training goals is up to the individual to tailor accordingly.

The training cycles are reasonably self-explanatory. They detail which weeks should include a particular set of programmes. As someone becomes more experienced with their own training, they may want to prioritise the areas at which they are weakest, or the programmes they find most challenging. Flexibility and cardiovascular exercise can take place continually throughout the year and complement the resistance training programmes.

If it is not possible to utilise even the abbreviated programme in its entirety, then it is best to begin as directed and work through the course until the skiing trip. This is far preferable to jumping the gun and beginning further along the course, or rushing through the earlier phases. If anything, the earlier phases are the most important for developing a solid base for skiing, and without that the rest is unlikely to be effective.

One thing that is not included in any part of the course is skiing on artificial slopes. This is because there are so many factors that may make this impractical. The entire course can be completed effectively at home with no need for travel, although recommendations have been made for those wishing to integrate this training with the equipment available in health clubs. Practising on an artificial slope would be of enormous value, particularly for novices who want to have a good idea of what they will encounter when going away to ski for the first time.

Novice to World Champion

This book and the exercise programmes are designed to make the human body a better unit for skiing. That means making it more resilient to muscle fatigue and injury, improving joint function, and improving the speed at which movements can be initiated and controlled. In all of these factors, it is irrelevant if the individual is a novice or a world champion because the point is not to improve technical skills but to improve the body in every way for skiing, including the ability to develop technical skills on the slopes. This means that everybody needs to begin at the beginning. Everyone can benefit from learning and training the proper and fine movements of the joints. From then on, the exercises become closer and closer to the real thing.

The difference between the novice and the world champion might be that an advanced skier wants to train faster, with more resistance, generating more power than a beginner. But the programmes themselves are the same, and the difference is purely in the specifics of how the individual adapts the exercises to the way in which they ski. If you do not ski, then take your time going through the movements, and make sure you are happy with what you are doing before moving on. If you are an advanced skier, then you will find many of the exercises quite straightforward but you have to try to put your mind into the exercise. You have to feel that the movements are replicating your movements when skiing, so as to ensure that you are training yourself specifically for skiing. For the novice, this will largely be guesswork, but the advanced skier should actually be able to *feel* the movement of the exercise in the same way that they *feel* the movement when skiing. Once that has been mastered, the next step is to increase speed and power so as to push the body and train it specifically for how you want to ski.

Exercise Terminology

While many clients have developed their own terminology to use during training sessions, the purpose of this section is to introduce the terminology specific to the training programme in this book.

- **Repetitions**, usually abbreviated to 'reps', refers to the number of times a particular movement is completed within a **set**. With squatting as an example (squatting is the movement of squatting down as if to sit on the floor and then standing back up again), the repetition is number of times that someone squats down and stands up before having a rest. That number then makes up one set. In most cases, the recommendation is to complete two or three sets, which does not include the one or two lighter 'warm-up' sets.
- The **rest** is the amount of time between sets and between exercises.
- **Frequency** refers to the number of days per week that the exercise, or programme, is to be performed.

Preferred training programme

	1	2	3	4	5	6	7	8	9	10	11	12	13	14	15	16	17	18
Training phase																		
Balance and proprioception																		
Muscular strength and endurance																		
Advanced joint strength and stability																		
Advanced muscular power																		
Advanced balance and proprioception																		
Flexibility																		
Cardiovascular																		

Preferred training programme Cont.

Training phase	19	20	21	22	23	24	25	26	27	28	29	30	31	32	33	34	35	36
Balance and proprioception																		
Muscular strength and endurance																		
Advanced joint strength and stability	■																	
Advanced muscular power			■	■	■	■	■	■	■	■								
Advanced balance and proprioception				■	■	■	■	■	■									
Flexibility	■	■	■	■	■	■	■	■	■	■	■	■	■	■	■	■	■	■
Cardiovascular																		

Abbreviated training programme

Training phase	1	2	3	4	5	6	7	8	9	10	11	12	13	14	15	16	17	18
Balance and proprioception	▓	▓																
Muscular strength and endurance			▓	▓	▓	▓												
Advanced joint strength and stability							▓	▓	▓	▓								
Advanced muscular power											▓	▓	▓					
Advanced balance and proprioception														▓	▓	▓		
Flexibility																		▓
Cardiovascular	▓	▓	▓	▓	▓	▓	▓	▓	▓	▓	▓	▓	▓	▓	▓	▓	▓	▓

Continued Training Programme

Training phase	1	2	3	4	5	6	7	8	9	10	11	12	13	14	15	16	17	18
Balance and proprioception	▓	▓	▓	▓														
Muscular strength and endurance									▓									
Advanced joint strength and stability										▓	▓	▓	▓	▓	▓	▓	▓	▓
Advanced muscular power																▓	▓	▓
Advanced balance and proprioception							▓											
Flexibility	▓	▓	▓				▓							▓	▓	▓	▓	▓
Cardiovascular	▓	▓	▓	▓	▓	▓	▓	▓	▓	▓	▓	▓	▓	▓	▓	▓	▓	▓

Continued Training Programme Cont.

Training phase	19	20	21	22	23	24	25	26	27	28	29	30	31	32	33	34	35	36
Balance and proprioception																		
Muscular strength and endurance																		
Advanced joint strength and stability																		
Advanced muscular power																		
Advanced balance and proprioception																		
Flexibility																		
Cardiovascular																		

	Continued Training Programme Cont.															
	37	38	39	40	41	42	43	44	45	46	47	48	49	50	51	52
Training phase																
Balance and proprioception																
Muscular strength and endurance																
Advanced joint strength and stability	▓	▓	▓										▓	▓	▓	
Advanced muscular power					▓	▓										
Advanced balance and proprioception									▓	▓	▓	▓				
Flexibility	▓	▓	▓	▓	▓	▓	▓	▓	▓	▓	▓	▓	▓	▓	▓	▓
Cardiovascular	▓	▓	▓	▓	▓	▓	▓	▓	▓	▓	▓	▓	▓	▓	▓	▓

This course of programmes recommends that resistance exercises are performed twice a week. This means that if a phase has one programme, then that programme should be repeated twice a week. If a phase has two programmes, then they should be completed once each in any particular week. If you feel adventurous and want to exercise three times a week, then alternate the programme you repeat twice.

As a worked example:

Exercise:	Squats
Reps:	10
Sets:	3
Rest:	30–60 seconds
Frequency:	1–2 days per week

So, you would warm-up by performing one or two sets of squats, through a reduced range of motion and at a slower pace. You would then perform 10 repetitions of squats, followed by a rest period of 30 to 60 seconds. You would then perform another 10 repetitions to make up the second set, have a rest, and then perform the final set of 10 repetitions, before moving on to the next exercise. More details about warming up and so on are included in the following sections.

It is important not to neglect the rest periods. If you do, the chances are that not enough effort is being put into the individual sets. The rest periods exist to allow energy levels to be replenished within the muscles, thereby making the following set more effective than if commencing it too early. Shorter rest periods confer some cardiovascular benefits, but at least 30 seconds is required to ensure that the muscles are capable of performing the subsequent set effectively. Rest periods of longer than a minute allow the heart rate to drop, and when considering what can be a high-intensity activity like skiing, it is better to aim for a shorter rather than longer break between sets.

Exercise Equipment

Various items of exercise equipment are featured throughout the exercise programmes. The equipment is recommended because it represents the best tools available for skiing training. The medicine balls are used because they are a convenient way of introducing more resistance to an exercise. A dumbbell, or pair of dumbbells, could be used in place of the medicine ball for many of the exercises, but for home training a medicine ball is far more versatile for these sorts of exercises. A 5-litre mineral water bottle could also be used in place of dumbbells and medicine balls, but because of the plastic they are less easy to prevent from slipping, so greater care is needed. If you try this and find yourself concentrating more on not dropping the water bottle on your head than you are on the exercise, it is time to make the investment!

Cable machines can be used in place of the resistance bands featured in some of the pictures. The bands cannot produce as much resistance as a cable machine in a gym, but if training at home then it is a perfectly good alternative. Another option is to train with someone who can mimic the resistance band by holding on to a towel and creating some manual resistance.

The Swiss ball is featured only once in the whole programme, and for a floor-based exercise at that. In this case, the Swiss ball creates a similar position to that encountered when lying on one's back and trying to manoeuvre the skis from facing one direction to facing the other, most often following a fall and attempting to get back up. It is better to get up facing across the slope rather than away from it, as you can then continue skiing rather than having to negotiate a static turn first. That one exercise could be performed without the Swiss ball, and by keeping the legs bent at 90 degrees in the hips and 90 degrees in the knees. This makes the movement much more difficult and places extra stress on the back. Stress, in this context, is necessary to cause the body to adapt.

The piece of equipment that looks like half a Swiss ball is called a BOSU, which stands for **BO**th **S**ides **U**p. This is much safer for standing on than a Swiss ball, although there are very few exercises that should be performed with the rounded side up. When skiing, it is necessary to lean into the slope. A similar position can be accomplished by placing one foot near the bottom, and one directly on top, of the BOSU. The BOSU is much more expensive than the Swiss ball due to the technology that goes into making them safe, and they are much more versatile.

The half-foam rolls that are used in this course are also a relatively new addition to the exercise trainer's arsenal. They are used primarily by physiotherapists and exercise therapists, and can be used for a number of exercises, muscle tests, and even for a sort of self-massage. They are quite inexpensive and allow for a wide range of stability exercises to be performed.

The purpose of the Swiss balls, BOSUs and foam rolls is to create instability. The goal is to perform exercises competently and effectively on a surface that is less stable than the floor. Although this would not be necessary for general resistance exercises in a gym, it becomes essential when training for an outdoor activity. When skiing, the ground is unpredictable and unstable. We cannot know how deep the snow is, whether it is likely to give way beneath our skis, if there is an ice patch or some sort of obstacle covered by the snow. Because of this, it is necessary to train the body in preparation.

Running outdoors creates similar stability dilemmas. Ice, mud, waterlogged ground, rocks, sand and snow all create problems that can throw a joint into an unnatural position. Training on an unstable surface therefore has great relevance for performance and injury prevention. The key is not to go overboard by training for stability that is not required. Many exercise instructors and personal trainers recommend performing exercises while seated on a Swiss ball to improve core stability. This is excessive because I for one never sit on anything unstable, and rarely need that added core stability to prevent me falling off my chair! Hence, with these tools we are in danger of getting into fashions rather than effective training, but all the exercises in this book facilitate training in a ski-specific position or posture.

All the exercise equipment featured in this book is available from:
www.thehealthybodyco.com

The Programmes

Warming Up

The warm-up is an essential and often neglected part of any exercise programme. The purpose of the warm-up is to increase blood flow to the working muscles and joints, which in turn delivers nutrients for energy and increases the elasticity of the muscles, improving performance and reducing the risk of injury. It is also important to warm-up to get the mind into the idea of doing exercise. The warm-up therefore has a cardiovascular (CV) component that involves increasing the heart rate and warming the muscles.

This cardiovascular component could be completed on any CV equipment in a gym, such as a bike or treadmill. Ideally, the CV machine should in some way replicate the movements of skiing, or at least be similar to the exercises in the main part of the programme. The cross-trainers or treadmills would be better than the rowing machines and bikes, if for no other reason than that they require the user to be standing rather than sitting. That should make sense, as sitting when skiing is the result of an accident or hot chocolate break, and there is certainly not going to be any sitting in the main programme.

If training at home, then it is best to mimic the exercises of the main workout, but starting off very gently and going through a much smaller range of motion. To mimic Split Squats (*see* page 65), begin in the same starting position, but bend the knees only a small amount at first, gradually increasing the range of motion until performing complete Split Squats. To mimic Forward Squats (*see* page 72), begin in the same position as for Squats, but again bend the knees and push the hips back only a small amount, and gradually increase the range of motion until squatting normally. The same principle works for Forward Lunges (*see* page 75), which could begin by just stepping forwards and then in various directions, gradually bringing in the knee bends until finally lunging normally. This should be repeated for all the exercises in the main programme, always beginning with a much-reduced range of motion, and starting slowly and gradually increasing speed until moving at a normal pace.

Ideally, the exercises of the warm-up would be mixed together so that you move from one exercise to the next at one speed and similarly reduced range of motion, and then repeat them in a sort of circuit format, but increasing speed and range of motion each time through. This takes some practice to make fluid but is probably the most efficient way of warming up, with the whole process taking anything from a few minutes upwards. Once the body is feeling warm and the joints comfortable with the movements, then the body is ready to move on to the next stage of the exercise programme.

The next stage in many exercise programmes is a mobility phase. This typically includes some light stretching and moving all the joints through a full range of motion. Stretching itself should really be avoided, unless instructed to do so by a physiotherapist or similar, as it relaxes the muscles and may actually increase the risk of injury. The exception to this is if a particular muscle is predisposed to injury, in which case a very thorough warm-up is required first, followed by specific stretching of the particular muscle, and then a reintroduction to the mimicking exercises of the warm-up. In most cases this would be at the advice of a physiotherapist or exercise scientist only.

The most important point of a mobility phase is to move the joints through the range of motion that will be demanded of them during the main exercises of the programme. This would already have been completed if following the home-based warm-up that avoids the use of cardiovascular equipment, and is based solely on preparing the body for the specific exercises of the programme. If using cardiovascular equipment, then the mobility phase of the warm-up can be introduced for each exercise of the main programme in turn. For example, when preparing to perform Squats, begin by using no extra resistance and moving slowly through a reduced range of motion. This should then be repeated at the beginning of each exercise, and will accomplish as much as the home-based warm-up.

The total length of the warm-up is dependent upon fitness levels and any other factors, such as health conditions. As a general rule, the fitter an individual, the less gradual and more demanding their warm-up should be. So, if a very fit and healthy person can complete a warm-up in about three minutes, then someone who is less accustomed to exercise or suffers from a particular health condition could spend anything up to 10 or 15 minutes warming up.

Fig 2.1 Torso Twists

Fig 2.2 Hip Flexors (Backward Lunges)

Fig 2.3 Squats with Front Raises

Fig 2.4 Adductors (Side Lunges)

General Points on Technique

For all the exercises in this book, unless stated otherwise, the basic technique principles are the same. The spine should maintain its normal curvature, and should not arch forwards or backwards or straighten. Although many people recommend a 'straight' back, they usually mean that it should maintain its natural curvature, or else they do not know very much about the spine. It took 10 million years to develop a spine as adept as ours for maintaining an upright posture and distributing stress throughout the body. Any deviation from this, including a 'straight' back, will increases stresses across the back and increase the risk of injury.

The hips should be kept level. For many of the exercises this may mean placing the hands on the top of the hips for the warm-up sets, just to check that the hips are doing what they are supposed to. The hips should not drop down on one side, move outwards or twist forwards or backwards. The pelvis should also be kept level to maintain the neutral spine, which means that it should not tilt in either direction. The only exception to the above is for rotational exercises, which will require twisting the hips, but they will be mentioned in turn.

The knees should always move in line with the second toe. In some exercises, the natural movement will allow the knees to pass over the toes, and this is important to balance out stresses on the spine. Some people advise against natural movements of the knee because of the stress that it causes to the joint, but this stress is usually equivalent only to that of walking. Furthermore, teaching the body to move unnaturally will affect the major joints across the whole body, and refer the stress to other joints such as the spine where it will have an even more profound effect.

The natural path of the knee should be over the middle of the foot (typically the second toe), while maintaining a neutral spine and correct hip position. The knees should therefore not track inwards or outwards, and a conscious effort may need to be made to correct this. Doing so will ultimately improve function and reduce stresses on the knee, which is obviously of great importance for skiing, where the natural movements require the knee to absorb and distribute various forces.

In the initial stages of the course, it may be necessary to spend longer on some of the early programmes to ensure that movements can be managed correctly. It is better to perform an exercise through a limited range of motion with good technique than to persevere with poor technique through a full range. A shorter range of motion can be developed over time, and you should progress to the next programme only when confident that all is correct.

In a standing posture, the feet can either be parallel, or one foot can be a few inches in front of the other (which reduces stress on the spine, but the hips should remain facing forwards). Unless otherwise stated, in static postures the knees and elbows should be slightly bent to allow muscles to be more involved in the distribution of stress than the bones themselves. When moving a particular joint, it should be straightened completely (although not beyond a straight line if you happen to have excessive range of motion in a particular joint). Moreover, all the postures and positions should be tailored to replicate the postures and positions utilised when skiing. This should not, however, detract from the general safety points of maintaining a neutral spine with slightly bent knees and elbows, and so on, unless specifically instructed to do so for a particular exercise.

With single leg movements, such as Single Leg Squats, the non-squatting leg can either be raised slightly to the front of the body, or else raised behind the body. Usually, the movement would involve raising the knee to the front, but because in skiing the leg doing the work is typically forward of the leg that is not (transiently, at least), it makes sense that in most of the exercises it is more specific to raise the leg to the back of the body.

General Pointers on the Programme

When beginning any exercise, it is important to perform one or two sets as warm-ups. This involves utilising a slower and steadier pace, and becoming confident with the technique and movement before making the exercise more demanding and dynamic. Warm-up sets are not included in the set count for each exercise programme, but one or two sets of 10 to 15 repetitions should be sufficient in each case.

Rest periods (given in seconds) refer to the maximum amount of time desirable between sets. Although for strength and power work it is normally preferable to have longer rest periods, because of the dynamics of skiing it is recommended to reduce otherwise optimal rest periods. The next set can commence as soon as the exerciser is comfortable to continue, and preferably well within the rest periods allocated, although this may need to be improved upon with training. Where numbers of sets and repetitions are given for exercises such as Single Leg Squats and Lunges, the numbers always refer to each leg, rather than an absolute total for both together.

The trend of the course is that each training phase is more demanding than the phase before. This is across many aspects of training, with more concentration and mental focus required on the later programmes to ensure proper technique. It is likely that these later training phases will also train the aerobic system (heart and lungs) more, as well as more of the muscles of the body to a greater extent. Therefore, all the way through the course it is necessary to perform the warm-ups and cool-downs as directed, and to develop these so that they fit in better with each programme. This is down to many individual factors, as well as the programme itself, and will not be easy to get right. Fitness instructors who teach classes spend a lot of time practising in front of mirrors at home and in the studio, and even then they can only produce a general programme that is not suited to everybody in the class. So it is unlikely that each programme will be perfect, but that will change over time with growing confidence, proficiency and some experimentation.

Balance and Proprioception

Basic Movement Skills: Weeks 1–4

- Single Leg Squats
- Split Squats
- Split Squats with Rotation (weeks 2–4 only).

When beginning an exercise programme for the first time, it is necessary to ensure that the joints are moving properly and that everything is in correct alignment. The reason for this is that although the main benefits of an exercise programme may come from big progressive exercises, there is little point starting off with a demanding programme only to become injured after a few months.

Our joints move most effectively and with minimal stress in a particular way. In early life, most people develop joints that move properly. However, certain factors can change the way a particular joint moves, such as wearing certain clothes, sports injuries or knocks from falls, or always carrying bags on one side. This may not produce noticeable changes at the time, but following repetitive movements such as running or resistance exercise – or even normal daily activities – sufficient wear and tear can eventually be produced on a joint to cause pain or injury.

In reality, people may exercise relatively injury- and pain-free for months or even years, despite having poor joint mechanics. Because of this, people may be causing damage to themselves without realising it. The damage may manifest itself as pain in the affected joint or another area of the body, and possibly increase the progression of degenerative conditions such as arthritis.

Proprioception refers to the body's ability to know where a particular body part is in space and time. It is the reason why you can move your arms or legs around with your eyes closed and still know where they are and what they are doing. On a finer scale, proprioception is how the brain and nervous system know when a limb is being moved and approaching a position where it is likely to get injured. If you stand on one foot with your eyes closed, then it is proprioception that helps to make the small corrections necessary to prevent you falling over (although there is also the interaction of other balance systems). So proprioception is vital for a fast-moving activity such as skiing, where the body needs to be trained in the various postures, and can make fast alterations and corrections when moving over a changing surface.

The purpose of this preliminary programme in basic movement skills is to spend a few weeks training the body to move the way that it is supposed to. Once this has been accomplished, you will have reduced the risk of joint problems, and improved the body's ability to cope with the more demanding aspects of the various exercise programmes. This basic programme can also be repeated if you start to experience joint pain in the future. The programme is unlikely to correct a joint problem completely, especially as this is a generalised, rather than individual, approach. The programme should, however, improve the way the joints work, and is better than simply beginning a more advanced routine without first teaching yourself the correct alignments of the joints.

Proprioception and Balance, Weeks 1–4

Exercise	Sets	Repetitions	Rest	Weeks
Single Leg Squats	3	10	90	1–4
Split Squats	3	10	90	1–4
Split Squats with Rotation	3	10	90	2–4

Single Leg Squats
(Legs, Butt, Calves)

This exercise has all the benefits of the standard squat, but performing the exercise on each leg independently is excellent for correcting any lower body imbalances. The Single Leg Squat can be performed with one foot raised slightly in front of the other, or else with one foot resting behind the body on a step or chair. Ensure that the knee travels forwards in line with the front of the foot, and does not move inwards or outwards. The pelvis should also be kept level and not allowed to dip down on either side.

Fig 2.5 Single Leg Squats

Split Squats
(Front of Thighs, Butt, Calves)

The Split Squat starts halfway through the lunge exercise. Begin by taking a large step forwards, as in the lunge, and then bend the front knee while dropping the back knee down to the floor. Return to the beginning by straightening the legs but keeping the feet in place. Ensure that the back remains upright throughout the exercise. Perform the exercise on one side for as many repetitions as necessary, then change so that the other foot is forwards.

Fig 2.6a Split Squats

Fig 2.6b Split Squats, with medicine ball

Split Squats with Rotation
(Legs, Calves, Torso)

This exercise is a combination of the split squat and rotation exercises. As the front leg bends, rotate the body so that the opposite shoulder turns towards the front knee. As the leg straightens back to the start position, bring the body back to facing forwards.

Fig 2.7a Split Squats with Rotation

Fig 2.7b Split Squats with Rotation, with medicine ball

Muscular Strength and Endurance

Secondary Movement Skills: Weeks 5–12

Programme 1
- Single Leg Squats
- Front Squats
- Box Squats
- Russian Twists
- Cable Two Arm Front Raise

Programme 2
- Split Squats
- Forward Lunges
- Side Lunges
- Backward Lunges
- Multidirectional Lunges
- Split Squats with Rotation (weeks 9–10 only)
- Lunges with Rotation (weeks 11–12 only)

Secondary movement skills are the first progression from the basic programme. By this stage the joints should be moving better than they were when you first started exercising. The attention paid to joint movements should be continued throughout the programmes, even more so as the programmes become more demanding.

The purpose of this part of the training is to develop muscular strength and endurance through a range of skiing-related exercises. As each programme develops, the movements become more similar to those involved in skiing. Each time, the basic movement is made more demanding, and for the health of the joints and efficiency of the muscles, it is important to master each aspect of the course before continuing to the next stage. Ideally, you should spend approximately eight weeks on these programmes to ensure that the movements have been mastered, and that the resistance used and the speed at which the exercises are performed can be improved.

The goal of the training course is to integrate muscular power with the body's ability to keep the joints in a safe position to prevent injury, and for the muscles to work effectively to maintain technique. Before developing power, it is first necessary to train the body in strength and endurance work. The exercises remain the same for both outcomes, but the way in which they are performed changes. The muscles of the body will change and make adaptations according to the specific stresses placed on them. Because of this, all the exercises replicate the movements of skiing to some degree, with the complexity increasing through the course of the programme.

Muscular endurance refers to the ability of the muscles to contract repeatedly for prolonged periods of time. When skiing down a slope, it is muscular endurance that allows the body to squat down and then push through each leg independently to allow for turns. The body is either holding a squat position, or is rising to prepare to push down through the inside edge of one foot and make a turn. At the same time, the torso twists towards the uphill leg/ski, the pole is planted in the snow, and the pressure through the downhill ski allows the turn to take place. The various muscles of the body are going through these phases throughout the downhill sections of the slope, with the energy required being reduced for flatter sections when holding a more static and upright posture. Even then, small corrections will constantly be made according to direction and changes in terrain.

In this part of the programme you must aim to perform each exercise at a similar speed to that you expect to move through when going down the slope. This is not power work, which will be rather fast, but more the steady pace you would adopt when going down a pleasant beginner's or intermediate slope.

Muscular power refers to the combination of strength and speed, but before progressing to that level of training, it is first necessary to train the muscles for strength. Muscular strength will also be useful when moving through more demanding sections of some courses, albeit still at a steady pace, and when manoeuvring around at the side of the slope.

There are two programmes in this phase of the course. Both are equally important and should be included in each week's training. The first programme includes squatting exercises to improve the body's ability to get into and rise out from tuck positions, and also to prepare for turns. There is also a rotational movement for the upper body, called Russian Twists, which improves the body's ability to twist in a good posture, and will help to protect the back from injury. The movement also replicates the motion of the upper body during a turn, as the torso twists to face into the slope as the pole is planted.

The final exercise on the first programme is a Two Arm Front Raise, using either a cable machine in a gym or resistance bands secured at a low level. The relevance of the exercise is to improve the body's ability to raise the arms out to the front of the body, which is important in preparation for planting poles during turns or for increasing speed. This is also the movement one is supposed to adopt if drifting backwards over the skis and about to fall. Quite handy then!

The second programme includes predominantly lunge-type exercises. These movements are important when walking with the skis, and also when pushing through one ski during turns. The various types of lunges also improve the body's ability to recover from skis going astray, and are intended not just to improve and correct technique but also to prevent injuries. The second programme also introduces more advanced rotational movements. This is again to develop the skills required for turning, and to improve the muscular strength and endurance required to do so. This should then improve efficiency on the slopes and reduce the risk of fatigue and injury.

Muscular Strength and Endurance, Weeks 5–12

Programme 1

Exercise	Sets	Reps	Rest	Weeks
(Endurance Phase)				
Single Leg Squats	3	15	30	5–8
Front Squats	2–3	15	30	5–8
Box Squats	2–3	15	30	5–8
Russian Twists	2–3	15	30	5–8
Cable Two Arm Front Raise	2–3	15	30	5–8
(Strength Phase)				
Single Leg Squats	3	10	90	9–12
Front Squats	2–3	10	90	9–12
Box Squats	2–3	10	90	9–12
Russian Twists	2–3	10	90	9–12
Cable Two Arm Front Raise	2–3	10	90	9–12

Muscular Strength and Endurance, Weeks 5–12

Programme 2

Exercise	Sets	Reps	Rest	Weeks
(Endurance Phase)				
Split Squats	2–3	15	30	5–8
Lunges	2–3	15	30	5–8
Side Lunges	2–3	15	30	5–8
Backward Lunges	2–3	15	30	5–8
Multidirectional Lunges	2–3	15	30	5–8
Split Squats with Rotation	2–3	15	30	5–8
Lunges with Rotation	2–3	15	30	5–8
(Strength Phase)				
Split Squats	2–3	10	90	9–12
Forward Lunges	2–3	10	90	9–12
Side Lunges	2–3	10	90	9–12
Backward Lunges	2–3	10	90	9–12
Multidirectional Lunges	2–3	10	90	9–12
Split Squats with Rotation	2–3	10	90	9–12
Lunges with Rotation	2–3	10	90	9–12

Programme 1

Single Leg Squats
This exercise is described in the previous section (*see* page 64).

Front Squats
The Front Squat is the same as a standard back squat, but with either the arms or a medicine ball held out in front of the body, or else a barbell or dumbbells positioned on the front of the shoulders. This position allows for a more upright posture during the movement, and is an excellent exercise for strengthening the muscles that stabilise the hips. If using a barbell, the arms should be crossed over, with the elbows kept slightly above shoulder height, so that the weight is supported by the shoulders rather than arms.

Fig 2.8 Front Squats

Box Squats
Box Squats are a standard back squat but with a much wider stance. The feet should be placed at greater than shoulder width apart, sufficient to elicit a slight stretch on the inner thighs during the movement. This trains the body to work when in a stretched position. As with Front Squats, this movement is excellent for strengthening the muscles that stabilise the pelvis.

Fig 2.9 Box Squats

Russian Twists

This movement can be completed with either a cable machine or a resistance band secured at mid-chest height. The stance should be wider than shoulder width, with the body at right angles to the cable or band. From there, twist towards the band or cable and move away from the band or cable so that you can feel the resistance. Then, keeping the arms stiff, twist the body away from the cable or band until you are facing the opposite direction. The movement should begin through quite a limited range of motion, with the hips facing forwards throughout, and the body weight distributed evenly on both feet. As you become more comfortable with the movement, allow the body weight to transfer from the foot nearest the cable or band to finish on the opposite foot when facing the other way. Hip and leg movement should be quite natural, permitting a greater range of motion, and utilising a steady tempo throughout the movement. This tempo can be developed over time to a more natural pace for skiing, but it is most important to be comfortable with the movement first, to ensure that the body is stable enough for the greater demands of a slightly faster and fuller movement.

Fig 2.10 Russian Twists

Cable Two Arm Front Raise

Stand forwards of the cable machine or site where the exercise bands are secured, so that the arms are extended slightly behind the body. With the arms slightly bent, raise them upwards in line with the shoulders. The movement should go as high as is comfortable (ideally as far as when raising the poles during skiing), and then return to the start position.

Fig 2.11 Cable Two Arm Front Raise

Programme 2

Split Squats

This exercise is described in the previous section (*see* page 65).

Forward Lunges

A lunge is just an extended step in a particular direction, usually followed by stepping back to the start position. Lunges can be performed in any direction, but we begin with a standard forward lunge. Take an exaggerated step forwards, planting the foot down and bending both knees (without allowing the back knee to touch the floor or the front knee to move excessively over the front foot). This is simply an exaggeration of a natural movement, and many people will do this when they pick something up from the floor when walking. If the knee does travel beyond the middle of the foot, then you might need to take a bigger stride or bend the back knee more (both knees should be close to 90 degrees). Once you have completed this first phase of the movement, then push back off the front foot to get back into the start position, and then repeat on the other leg.

Fig 2.12 Forward Lunges

Side Lunges

The concept for this movement is the same as for the Forward Lunge. This time the movement is directly out to the side of the body and back, keeping both feet pointing forwards, and only bending the leg that moves out to the side (this allows for a slight stretch on the inside of the other leg). Alternate which foot moves out to the side, and which stays in place.

Fig 2.13 Side Lunges

Backward Lunges

This version of the lunge requires a little more practice to get right as the step is behind the body, so you cannot see where you are planting your foot. As the foot moves back, the balls of the foot touch the ground and then both knees bend, and then return to the start position and repeat on the other side. You can alternate between pushing off from both legs, just the back leg and just the front leg. All are useful movements and are involved in skiing.

Fig 2.14 Backward Lunges

Multidirectional Lunges

Multidirectional Lunges can be completed in a number of ways. You can either imagine a clock face, or else just come up with random patterns, but the idea is that you move in any direction, including with one leg crossed over the front of the other (although much more care is needed). Utilise forward, backward, sideways, diagonal and crossover lunges, and work until you feel you have worked your

Fig 2.15 Multidirectional Lunges

legs from every angle. As long as the knee does not move excessively over the foot, the hips remain relatively stable, the back remains mostly neutral, and you do not feel that you are going to hurt yourself, then you are doing a good job.

Split Squats with Rotation (weeks 5–6 only)
This exercise is described in the previous section (*see* page 66).

Lunges with Rotation (weeks 7–12 only)
This exercise is a standard Forward Lunge, but twisting towards the leg that moves forwards. This is simply a more dynamic version of the Split Squat with Rotation, utilising more speed and power, and helping to create a more natural movement when skiing. Try to keep the hips level. Twist comfortably, beginning slowly and increasing speed to a more natural pace when ready. If using a medicine ball, be sure that you are controlling the movement, and do not use momentum at this stage as you are unlikely to have the stability to control it effectively.

Fig 2.16 Lunges with Rotation

Advanced Joint Strength and Stability

Tertiary Movement Skills: Weeks 13–20

Programme 1
- Alternate Single Leg Squats with Tuck
- Front Squats with Behind the Head Reach
- Alternate Single Leg Squats with Internal Rotation
- Hip Adduction with Single Leg Squats (band at 45 degrees behind outside leg)
- Pull-downs with Squats
- Single Arm Pull-downs with Single Leg Squats
- Swiss Ball Pelvic Twists (Knee Rocks)

Programme 2
- Step-ups
- Reverse Step-ups
- Side Step-ups
- Lunges with Rotation
- Multidirectional Lunges with Rotation
- Wood Chops (Single Arm) with Squats
- Cable Two Arm Front Raise with Squats
- Cable Two Arm Front Raise with Lunges

As with the previous phase, this third phase of developing movement skills also comprises two programmes. Both programmes are a development of the two in the previous phase, with movements requiring much greater control, coordination and concentration in order to perform the exercises correctly. Again, these exercises are much closer to the actual movements of skiing than the ones in the previous two programmes.

This phase of the programme introduces a quite specialised movement in the form of a Tuck Squat. Throughout the programmes so far, the technique used in squatting has been precisely that required for proper movement. It is the same squat that you did when you first learned to stand up, and the same squat that many people do if they sit on the floor more than they sit in chairs. That normal squatting movement is usually distorted as an effect of muscular imbalances or injuries, or through being taught the wrong way to squat in exercise classes and so on.

Professional jockeys are taught to adopt a 'Martini glass posture' when racing. This means that there is a straight line from the ankles to the knees, which is perpendicular to the ground. There is then a 45-degree line from the knees to the hips, and an invisible 45-degree line from the knees to the shoulders. This is not by any means a sound posture to adopt unless it is required, as is the case for jockeys.

In skiing, the tuck position requires a slightly lopsided Martini glass. Ideally, the knees would be positioned slightly forward of the toes, but this position is not possible due to the restricted movement within the ski boots. Although the hips have to be positioned behind the knees, the body weight is kept forward to aid control and balance. The back also tends to be rounded, although this should be minimised as much as possible, depending upon how much flexibility there is in the back of the legs (hamstrings). Because the torso is perpendicular to the lower legs, it is necessary to tilt the head back in order to see what is ahead down the slope. Over a prolonged period, this will lead to neck discomfort and pain, so you should try to tilt the head as little as possible while almost looking through your eyebrows.

The purpose of this book is to train people for skiing, but the dilemma here is that the tuck position is not by any means a good posture to maintain for any length of time. The position is included in this phase, but more as a transitional movement while going through Single Leg Squats and so on, again replicating its actual involvement in skiing. Many normal squatting movements have been included to ensure that you will not learn to use the Tuck Squat in place of a normal Squat, and so that you will have the ability to perform all the required movements for skiing.

The second exercise is the Front Squat with Behind the Head Reach. The purpose of this exercise is to help teach the body to come into a forward position when the torso is extending backwards. This movement is therefore useful for improving balance when skiing and helping to prevent falling over the back of the skis.

The Single Leg Squats with Rotation are another progression of the original Split Squats with Rotation. This exercise will improve the body's efficiency and accuracy for turns. The Hip Adduction with Single Leg Squats is to help ensure that you can control where the skis are, and prevent them from drifting out to the sides. This may also prove useful for control over patches of ice, when it is necessary to either change weight distribution or control the skis better. The introduction of the Pull-down exercises is to train the muscles required for planting the ski poles during turns, or for producing more forward propulsion off the poles.

The Swiss Ball Pelvic Twists (or 'Knee Rocks', as my chief scientific adviser John Hardy suggested) were included following a flash of inspiration. Swiss Balls are far too overused in many exercise programmes, and their actual relevance is nearly always minimal. This exercise has absolutely no use save for the use for which it was included in this programme. Should you fall over, then it is necessary to get the skis pointing across the slope, as if you try to get up while the skis are pointing down the slope then you tend to fall over again quite abruptly. Manoeuvring the skis often also includes twisting the hips so that the skis are pointing in the opposite direction (across the slope rather than off the side of it). The manoeuvring required is very similar to this exercise using the Swiss Ball, with even the height of the ball being similar to that gained from the back of the skis. This exercise may therefore save much effort from being expended when compared to encountering this position for the first time on the slopes. It is bad enough falling over, but even worse not to be able to get up again easily afterwards.

The second programme begins with different versions of Step-ups. These have good practical relevance for moving around the side of the slopes, for side-stepping when a beginner, getting into a good start position, and for stepping up the slope to retrieve a lost ski pole. The Step-ups and Reverse Step-ups in particular are also good for promoting correct knee and hip movements.

The Lunges with Rotation are also useful for skiing and turning. The Wood Chops are a progression from the Russian Twists, and again are closer to the actual muscle involvement in various twisting manoeuvres during skiing. The two variations of the Two Arm Cable Raises are in preparation for turns and propulsion. The squat and lunge movements make this original exercise more appropriate to how the movement is actually used when skiing.

Advanced Joint Strength and Stability: Weeks 13–20

Programme 1

Exercise	Sets	Reps	Rest
Alternate Single Leg Squats with Tuck	2	8	60
Front Squats with Behind the Head Reach	2	8	60
Alternate Single Leg Squats with Internal Rotation	2	8	60
Hip Adduction with Single Leg Squats	2	8	60
Pull-downs with Squats	2	8	60
Single Arm Pull-downs with Single Leg Squats	2	8	60
Swiss Ball Pelvic Twists (Knee Rocks)	2	8	60

Advanced Joint Strength and Stability: Weeks 13–20

Programme 2

Exercise	Sets	Reps	Rest
Step-ups	2	8	60
Reverse Step-ups	2	8	60
Side Step-ups	2	8	60
Lunges with Rotation	2	8	60
Multidirectional Lunges with Rotation	2	8	60
Single Arm Wood Chops	2	8	60
Cable Two Arm Front Raise with Squats	2	8	60
Cable Two Arm Front Raise with Lunges	2	8	60

Programme 1

Alternate Single Leg Squats with Tuck

This is a standard single leg squat but involves alternating the legs from one side to the other. At the bottom of the squat position, the back/torso should be rounded forwards into a 'tuck' position for skiing. This allows the body to replicate this particular skiing posture, while going through similar leg movements required for turning and varying ground conditions, such as ice and bumps.

Fig 2.17 Alternate Single Leg Squats with Tuck

Front Squats with Behind the Head Reach

This is a medicine ball movement, starting with the ball held out in front during the downward phase of the squat, and then reaching the ball up above and slightly behind the head on the upward phase. Actual range of motion is dependent upon shoulder and core strength. This exercise should be performed slowly at first, with both range of motion and speed increased gradually as the body becomes stronger and more stable with the movement. The head should remain in line with the upper body during the movement (so if the arms go a

Fig 2.18 Front Squats with Behind the Head Reach

reasonable distance behind the body, the head and neck should also be leaning back slightly, rather than straining to stay looking forwards).

Alternate Single Leg Squats with Internal Rotation

As with the first exercise in this programme, this also involves a standard single leg squat, which then alternates between sides on each repetition. The difference is that this time the body should be twisted, so that the second foot is placed down at right angles to the first, as if stepping around two sides of a square. The next repetition then twists back to the start position. The twist comes from the hips, with the squat pushing down straight through the hip, knee and ankle (there is no twisting once the foot has been placed). This is a similar movement to that required for turns on the slope.

Fig 2.19 Alternate Single Leg Squats with Internal Rotation

Hip Adduction with Single Leg Squats
(band at 45 degrees behind outside leg)

This unusual movement requires an exercise band or cable with ankle attachment to complete effectively. The band/cable should be attached to one ankle so that there is a line of 45 degrees out behind the leg towards the band attachment/cable machine. The legs should be at a similar width apart, as for Box Squats (*see* page 72). The leg with the band/cable then moves to be right next to the other leg, and you should perform a single leg squat (the free leg is therefore raised during the squat and planted again before the other leg moves back to the start position). This exercise is to help train the body to work when resisting backward forces (typically momentum, although a small obstacle could have the same result on the slope).

Fig 2.20 Hip Adduction with Single Leg Squats

Pull-downs with Squats

This exercise should be performed facing a cable machine, or with a band secured in the middle above head height. The arms should be pulled down to the sides of the body and slightly back. The arms should start off bent, straighten during the movement until they are completely straight, then return to the start position. You should descend into the squat position as the arms come down so that the arms are back and straight when at the bottom of the squat.

Fig 2.21 Pull-downs with Squats

Single Arm Pull-downs with Single Leg Squats

This movement is similar to the above but uses a single leg squat while performing a single arm pull-down with the opposite side. This one may be a feat of coordination, so you might want to get one side right before changing to the other. The goal, however, is to be able to alternate from one leg to the other, while at the same time alternating between opposite arms.

Fig 2.22 Single Arm Pull-downs with Single Leg Squats

Swiss Ball Pelvic Twists (Knee Rocks)

Begin by lying on your back with your calves and ankles on top of the ball. The arms should be out to the side of the body and resting on the floor for stability. The movement is then a slight rock of the hips, allowing the feet to roll the ball from one side to the other. Gradually increase the range of motion, but keep the back relatively flat on the floor, with the head down, and always

Fig 2.23 Swiss Ball Pelvic Twists (Knee Rocks)

perform the movement in a steady manner. This is purely to improve recovery following falls, so in real life you might be lucky to test the effectiveness of this exercise once or twice at the most, perhaps more if you are a beginner or just into testing yourself.

Programme 2

Step-ups

Begin by facing a step, then raise one foot and place it in the middle of the step so that neither the front nor back of the foot is hanging off. Bring the other foot up alongside the first, and then step back in the same order. On the next step-up, alternate which side leads so as to keep everything even. The head position should be forward, helping to maintain the neutral spine, but glance down to check that the knee is moving forwards of the middle of the foot rather than in or out. At the same time, the hips should be level rather than tilted downwards or twisting forwards or backwards. If this does occur, slow the movement down and concentrate on keeping everything in good alignment.

Fig 2.24 Step-ups

Reverse Step-ups

As the name suggests, this is basically the opposite of a standard step-up but allows for much greater care in maintaining correct alignment. Begin at the top of the step, with one foot hanging off the back. Concentrate on the supporting leg, maintaining level hips and ensuring the knee travels directly forwards over the middle of the foot. Slowly bend the supporting knee and allow the other foot to descend towards the floor, but bring it up to the start position rather than allowing it to rest on the floor.

Fig 2.25 Reverse Step-ups

Side Step-ups

This mimics the action of side steps up a ski slope. This is an integral part of a beginner's skiing programme and important for anyone wanting to position themselves a little higher up the slope or else to retrieve wayward poles. Standing side-on to the step, raise the leg nearest to it and plant the foot flat down in the centre of the step. Raise the other leg and bring it alongside the first before stepping down onto the other side of the step, and then repeating. Make sure that the whole foot comes to rest on the step, and that the foot is placed in the centre of the step rather than precariously off to one side.

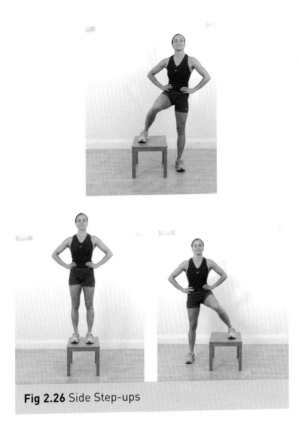

Fig 2.26 Side Step-ups

Lunges with Rotation

This exercise is a standard forward lunge, but twisting towards the leg that moves forwards. This is simply a more dynamic version of the Split Squat with Rotation (*see* page 66), utilising more speed and power, and helping to create a more natural movement when skiing. Try to keep the hips level. Twist comfortably, beginning slowly and increasing speed to a more natural pace when ready. If using a medicine ball, be sure that you are controlling the movement, and do not use momentum at this stage as you are unlikely to have the stability yet to control it effectively.

Fig 2.27 Lunges with Rotation

Multidirectional Lunges with Rotation

This is a progression of standard Lunges with Rotation (*see* above). As you work through a set of multidirectional lunges, twist the torso in the direction of the leading leg. There may be some movements for which this feels unnatural, such as crossover or backward lunges, but work out for yourself in which direction the twist feels best for each direction of lunge, or vary between both sides. Start off slowly and deliberately, as you get used to combining the two movements, and gradually increase to a more natural pace as you become more confident and comfortable.

Fig 2.28 Multidirectional Lunges with Rotation

Single Arm Wood Chops

This movement is a progression of the Russian Twists (*see* page 73). The cable or band should be set at above shoulder height. Stand sideways on to the cable/band and hold on to it by reaching across with the opposite hand. Twist the body (as for Russian Twists) but allow the arm to finish in the opposite position to where it started (opposite side of the body and lower than the hips). The arm should be kept stiff all the way through the movement. Integrate a squat so that you bend your knees as the arm comes across and down, and then stand up as the arm returns to the start position. The hips should be kept relatively stable, with the knees moving normally and therefore resisting any excessive twisting movements associated with what the torso is doing (some is natural, but the twisting movement should be lead from the torso rather than all from the hips).

Fig 2.29 Single Arm Wood Chops

Cable Two Arm Front Raise with Squats

This exercise is a development of the Cable Two Arm Front Raise used in an earlier programme (*see* page 74). This time, begin in the bottom position of a squat with the arms out behind the body to grasp the cable/band, and the body again positioned to be facing away from the cable/band. As you come up out of the squat, raise the arms to complete the front raise, and then return to the start position. This exercise can be performed well with a medicine ball in a similar fashion, although the resistance will be through a slightly limited range of motion.

Fig 2.30 Cable Two Arm Front Raise with Squats

Cable Two Arm Front Raise with Lunges

This movement is similar to the exercise above, but this time you perform the front raise while doing a forward lunge. Again, cables and bands are good and allow for a better range of motion, but a medicine ball is certainly adequate. Ensure that you do not lean back

Fig 2.31 Cable Two Arm Front Raise with Lunges

excessively as the arms pass shoulder level, as this may compromise the lower back. This should not occur if the movement is performed slowly and comfortably while getting used to it.

Muscular Power

Advanced Power Skills: Weeks 21–28

- Forward Lunges
- Power Lunges
- Power Split Squats
- Power Lunges with Rotation
- Power Split Squats with Rotation
- Jumping Squats
- Jumping Front Squats (with Medicine Ball)
- Jumping Front Squats with Rotation (90 degrees)

Skiing proficiently, safely and efficiently involves a number of factors. Balance and proprioception are key to preventing falls and injuries. Muscular endurance is key to preventing muscular fatigue. Muscular power, however, is what ensures muscles initiate sufficient forces to turn fast, to jump and to work in conjunction with balance and proprioception to prevent injuries at even the fastest speeds. Muscular power is necessary on all slopes because the body nearly always needs to integrate its strength with speed to move and react as required, and is essential on the tougher intermediate and all advanced slopes. Power is also required, in differing amounts, when skiing in the steeper or softer slopes off-piste.

The exercises in this phase may not seem as technical as the ones in the previous phases. This is because there are fewer exercises and they are progressions of otherwise quite basic movements. However, the amount of concentration required – in ensuring that the hips remain level, the knees are moving in line with the second toe and that the back retains its neutral curvature during the jumping exercises – is far greater than that required in previous phases. While it is possible to forget about all that and just get on with the exercises, this could undo a lot of the work put in so far to ensure correct movement and joint alignment.

The development of power at this stage, particularly in the form of jumping movements, is essential for advanced skiing techniques. Having that power available, however, is just as necessary for preventing injuries on the gentler slopes. There will always be fleeting moments when the skis are pointing in the wrong direction, when some evasive action has left you out of space, or when another user of the slope has knocked you or you have gone over some ice or a concealed obstacle. When that happens, it is the ability of the muscles to react accordingly, and at speed, that prevents a fall or an accident. The impact of these exercises will also strengthen the joints to help prevent injuries caused by repetitive impacts or joint movements on the slopes.

Advanced Power Skills: Weeks 21–28

Exercise	Sets	Reps	Rest
Forward Lunges	1–2	6	60
Power Lunges	1–2	6	60
Power Split Squats	1–2	6	60
Power Lunges with Rotation	1–2	6	60
Power Split Squats with Rotation	1–2	6	60
Jumping Squats	1–2	6	60
Jumping Front Squats (with Medicine Ball)	1–2	6	60
Jumping Front Squats with Rotation (90 Degrees)	1–2	6	60

Lunges
This exercise is described in a previous section (*see* 'Forward Lunges', page 75).

Power Lunges
This movement is the same as for standard Forward Lunges (*see* page 75), but a more forceful push-off is required from the front foot. This is to generate more power through the hip and leg in this position, so the aim is to complete a full movement but to return to the start position as quickly as possible.

Fig 2.32 Power Lunges

Power Split Squats
This movement is similar to standard Split Squats (*see* page 65). This time, however, you should generate sufficient force through both legs on the way up so that you can alternate the front leg in the air, and then perform a Power Split Squat on the other side, and so on. This is a continuous and very fast exercise where you jump at the top of the movement, switch leg positions and keep repeating the movement on one side and then the other.

Fig 2.33 Power Split Squats

Power Lunges with Rotation

This movement is the same as for standard Forward Lunges with Rotation (*see* page 78), but again producing as much power as possible through the front leg, thereby completing the full movement with rotation much faster than with the standard movement.

Fig 2.34 Power Lunges with Rotation

Power Split Squats with Rotation

By this stage in the course, you should have developed the speed, strength and stability to perform this exercise safely and effectively. The key is still to get the movement right before developing speed and power. Perform a Power Split Squat (*see* above) and rotate as with the standard rotation exercises. Be aware of the position of the spine and hips, and try to avoid allowing the hips to drop down or twist forwards excessively. Practise a few repetitions of Power Split Squats before introducing the rotation. The rotation should be towards the leg that moves forwards. This is very dynamic movement because the forward leg switches quickly between each repetition.

Fig 2.35 Power Split Squats with Rotation

Jumping Squats

This movement is a Forward Squat (*see* page 72) but with acceleration on the upward phase. The acceleration should be sufficient to allow for a jump straight upwards. When the feet touch the ground, be sure to absorb the energy of the landing by bending the hips and knees sufficiently. In fact, you should allow that bending to be the first part of the downward phase of the next repetition. Again, this is a very dynamic exercise, and if you start getting tired it is better to rest rather than risk allowing technique to deteriorate.

Jumping Front Squats (with Medicine Ball)
This movement is similar to Jumping Squats (*see* above), but this time holding a medicine ball in front of the chest. Vary the distance from the chest as a progression of the exercise, but be aware that the further the ball is from the chest, the greater the stress put on the lower back. If you do want to hold the ball a significant distance away from the chest, it is advisable to bring it in for the landing phase of the movement.

Fig 2.36 Jumping Front Squats (with Medicine Ball)

Jumping Front Squats with Rotation (90 Degrees)
This movement is the same as the Jumping Front Squats (*see* above) but with the ball held close to the chest throughout, and then jumping so that you twist and land at 90 degrees to where you started, and then jump back. You should naturally try to jump off from the outside leg a little more than the inside leg, both to make the rotation work and to make the movement more similar to fast turns when skiing.

Fig 2.37 Jumping Front Squats with Rotation (90 degrees)

Advanced Balance and Proprioception

Advanced Movement Skills: Weeks 29–36

Programme 1
- Single Leg Hops
- Lateral Hops to Single Leg Squats
- Twisting Hops to Single Leg Squats
- BOSU Squats (Flat Side Up)

- BOSU Squats (Round Side Up and Off-centre)
- BOSU Squats (Flat Side Up and Off-centre)
- Jumping BOSU Squats (Flat Side Up)
- Jumping BOSU Squats (Round Side Up and Off-centre)
- Jumping BOSU Squats (Flat Side Up and Off-centre)

Programme 2
- Front Squats
- Half-foam Roll Squats (1 Foot on, 1 Foot on Floor, Varying Angles)
- 2 x Half-foam Roll Squats (Both Feet in Varying Angles)
- Half-foam Roll Split Squats (Varying Angles)
- Single Leg Half-foam Roll Squats (Maintain Position)
- Wood Chops (Single Arm) with Single Leg Squats
- Alternate Single Leg Squats with Tuck on BOSU (Flat Side Up)
- Alternate Single Leg Squats with Tuck on BOSU (Round Side Up)

This final programme is the culmination of all the skills developed thus far. Balance and proprioception are now developed further, integrating the improved joint strength and muscular endurance with the power developed in the latest phase of the course. These exercises are the most demanding of all the programmes, and once completed with competence, it is reasonable to suppose that overall injury risk will have been reduced, and skiing ability itself will have the capacity to be improved. These exercises should be sufficient to test the most seasoned professional, and in doing so will ensure that all skiers, from absolute beginners upwards, are better prepared for the slopes.

Staying upright is all about how the muscles work to maintain balance and make corrections according to proprioception. When skiing, the ground can be read by looking at it, but the softness of the snow, the existence of ice and any obstacles beneath the snow will not be known until the skis have already touched them. At this point the skier is entirely reliant on their balance and proprioception to know how to correct themselves and prevent a fall or make a turn. Good balance and proprioception when static on the ground is of little relevance when moving or on an unstable or unpredictable surface, which is when muscular power is integrated. This is not just about the big squatting-type movements that have been practised so far; it is also about the small movements around all the joints of the body to bring everything back into correct alignment. This principle underlies the importance of such a thorough and comprehensive set of programmes.

If someone can perform all these exercises, then there is little more of relevance that can be used to challenge them in preparation for skiing. The use at this stage of various movements on the BOSU and foam rolls is to ensure that the body can perform all the movements of skiing, even when thrown into an otherwise unusual position. So the point of this part of the course is to develop balance and proprioception further, as well as joint strength and muscular power, while moving the joints through various positions relevant to skiing. Keeping this in mind, the point of each exercise should be clear.

Because there are so many different positions that might be encountered when skiing, it is advisable to move the foam rolls around to test the body in as many different positions as possible. The speed, sets and repetitions, and rest periods should all be varied, so as to develop all aspects of muscle function. This might include some high-repetition work for endurance, lower repetitions for strength, and lower repetitions and higher speed for power. Always begin by improving competence at endurance work before progressing to the more demanding work required of strength and power exercises.

Finally, the exercises in these two programmes are more advanced than those encountered by many accomplished exercise professionals. The reason for this is to ensure that the body is properly trained to react when necessary to the conditions of the skiing sessions. Because the programme is so advanced, it is essential that you have prepared for it by completing all the other programmes up to this point in their entirety. You should then begin the movements of these two programmes in a steady and controlled manner before increasing speed to progress to a more natural skiing pace.

Advanced Movement Skills: Weeks 29–36

Programme 1

Exercise	Sets	Reps	Rest
Single Leg Hops	2–3	6	45
Lateral Hops to Single Leg Squats	2–3	6	45
Twisting Hops to Single Leg Squats	2–3	6	45
BOSU Squats (Flat Side Up)	2–3	6	45
BOSU Squats (Round Side Up and Off-centre)	2–3	6	45
BOSU Squats (Flat Side Up and Off-centre)	2–3	6	45
Jumping BOSU Squats (Flat Side Up)	2–3	6	45
Jumping BOSU Squats (Round Side Up and Off-centre)	2–3	6	45
Jumping BOSU Squats (Flat Side Up and Off-centre)	2–3	6	45

Advanced Movement Skills: Weeks 29–36

Programme 2

Exercise	Sets	Reps	Rest
Front Squats	2–3	6	45
Half-foam Roll Squats (1 Foot on, 1 Foot on Floor, Varying Angles)	2–3	6	45
2 x Half-foam Roll Squats (Both Feet in Varying Angles)	2–3	6	45
Half-foam Roll Split Squats (Varying Angles)	2–3	6	45
Single Leg Half-foam Roll Squats (Maintain Position)	2–3	6	45
Wood Chops (Single Arm) with Single Leg Squats	2–3	6	45
Alternate Single Leg Squats with Tuck on BOSU (Flat Side Up)	2–3	6	45
Alternate Single Leg Squats with Tuck on BOSU (Round Side Up)	2–3	6	45

Programme 1

Single Leg Hops

A hop is the progression of a Single Leg Squat (*see* page 64). Begin by performing the downward phase of a Single Leg Squat, and generate sufficient force to allow the foot the leave the ground. As with Jumping Squats (*see* page 100), it is important to absorb the landing by bending at the hips and knees, and then use this as the beginning of the next repetition.

Fig 2.38 Single Leg Hops

Lateral Hops to Single Leg Squats

A Lateral Hop is a standard hop but out to the side and then back to the start position. The addition of the Single Leg Squat is to add a control element to the movement. Hop out to the side, then as you absorb the landing, perform a standard Single Leg Squat (*see* page 64), and then perform a hop back to the start position.

Fig 2.39 Lateral Hops to Single Leg Squats

Twisting Hops to Single Leg Squats

The movement is similar to the previous exercise, but when you jump the body should twist so that the foot is then planted at 90 degrees to where it started. Perform the Single Leg Squat (*see* page 64) and then hop back to the start position. Because the movement is quite difficult to master, it may be best to perform the exercise on one side and then alternate, rather than alternate for each repetition.

Fig 2.40 Twisting Hops to Single Leg Squats

BOSU Squats (Flat Side Up)

This is a progression of the Forward Squat (*see* page 72) but using the BOSU to make the movement less stable, which requires the body to stabilise in order to perform the exercise correctly. A common mistake is to use stabilisation exercises before the body is ready for them, in which case you may only be training imbalances. For this reason, it is important to perform the exercises slowly at first, with the feet wide on the flat surface of the BOSU, and maintaining a level surface.

Fig 2.41 BOSU Squats (Flat Side Up)

BOSU Squats (Round Side Up and Off-centre)

This exercise is similar to squatting on the flat surface, but slightly better suited to the positions required to work through when skiing. Place one foot just off the centre of the BOSU, and the other close to the edge. You should be able to lean the body across the BOSU, with the outside of the upper foot and inside of the lower foot pressing into the BOSU. This squatting position is very similar to that required for cutting into the sides of the slope when parallel skiing (a bigger BOSU would be better for a wider, more stable stance, but they do not exist, and buying two BOSUs for one exercise would prove somewhat less than cost-effective). The knees should still travel forwards, although the hips have to push towards the centre of the BOSU to maintain a stable position.

Fig 2.42 BOSU Squats (Round Side Up and Off-centre)

BOSU Squats (Flat Side Up and Off-centre)

This exercise replicates the above but with a less stable surface. By using the flat side, the tendency is for the BOSU to pivot over the centre, which needs to be controlled during the movement. This added balance requirement is sufficient to elicit improvement in balance similar to that required when skiing fast over an unpredictable surface. Start by performing the squats slowly, and getting used to how the BOSU tends to move when squatting on it, before progressing to a more natural pace.

Jumping BOSU Squats (Flat Side Up)

Although the word 'jumping' is used, it is much more of a 'lift' of momentum, rather than an actual jump with the whole body leaving the BOSU. Begin by just transferring the body weight onto the balls of the feet as the heels rise at the top of the movement. If the feet leave the BOSU completely, it should be relatively slowly

Fig 2.43 BOSU Squats (Flat Side Up and Off-centre)

and travelling only an inch or so above the BOSU, concentrating particularly on ensuring a safe landing. The movement is very appropriate for jumping and landing when skiing, but there are risks both in skiing and training, and this should only be attempted if you are likely to utilise ski jumps when on the slopes. The landing on the BOSU should replicate a proper landing, with a good bend in the hips and knees, a slightly forward body position, with the hands slightly out to the front.

Fig 2.44 Jumping BOSU Squats (Flat Side Up)

Jumping BOSU Squats (Round Side Up and Off-centre)

This movement is the progression of the BOSU squats with the round side up and off-centre. The movement should be practised for the first few repetitions without the jump, just to ensure correct foot and body position, and then gradually increase the speed, again only allowing the feet to travel an inch or so off the surface of the BOSU.

Fig 2.45 Jumping BOSU Squats (Round Side Up and Off-centre)

Jumping BOSU Squats (Flat Side Up and Off-centre)
This movement is the progression of the BOSU squats with the flat side up and off-centre. This time the movement is really to lift the body up, without any necessity to take the feet off the BOSU, but instead to simply transfer body weight from one foot to the other. This means that the body will desend into a squat, then as you come up the momentum of the movement takes your weight away from your feet, and then you press down through one side and go back down into a squat. During the next repetition the body weight is transferred to the opposite leg and so on. This BOSU will therefore tilt from one side to the other, replicating the forces and movements through the lower limbs that are associated with parallel turns when skiing. The movement is particularly good for training the muscles that support the ankles when jumping and turning at speed when skiing, but the initial training has to be very controlled and deliberate.

Fig 2.46 Jumping BOSU Squats (Flat Side Up and Off-centre)

Programme 2

Front Squats
This exercise is described in a previous section (*see* 'Front Squats', page 72).

Half-foam Roll Squats
(1 Foot on, 1 Foot on Floor, Varying Angles)

The half-foam roll is an excellent tool for developing stability across a number of joints in the body. As with the BOSU, this is quite challenging, and it is important to work through the movements slowly and deliberately, only progressing to a more natural pace when controlled and confident enough to do so. This exercise is basically like a Front Squat but with a wide (skiing-width) stance, and one foot placed on the flat side of the half-foam

Fig 2.47 Half-foam Roll Squats

roll. Once you can squat comfortably with the foam roll staying relatively still, the movement can be progressed to allow the squats to occur with the foam roll tilted slightly inwards or outwards. This better replicates the stability needs of skiing, but it is important that the movements are controlled throughout, with both knees travelling forwards over the centre of the foot and the normal backward motion of the hips.

2 x Half-foam Roll Squats (Both Feet in Varying Angles)

This is the same as the previous exercise, but with both feet on half-foam rolls. Once competent at performing the exercise with the flat sides of the foam roll staying in position all the way through, the movement can be progressed to allow the foam rolls to tilt. Aim to perform the squat with the foam rolls held in the tilted position throughout. As with skiing, the foam rolls should be tilted in the same direction and at the same angle, either both to the left or both to the right.

Fig 2.48 2 x Half-foam Roll Squats (Both Feet in Varying Angles)

Half-foam Roll Split Squats (Varying Angles)

This movement is more demanding than the parallel squats, as the narrower stance decreases stability. There is a technique in some types of skiing which utilises a similar movement, although it can happen by accident, and training for this position may help avert a fall. Place the foam rolls on the floor with the flat sides up in an appropriate position for split squats. The majority of the repetitions should be performed with the flat sides up and stabilised all the way through. A few repetitions should be practised with the tops of the foam rolls tilted to one side or the other. The exercise should be performed slowly at first, especially with consideration to the greater stabilisation requirements of this movement, but then progressed to a natural up and down tempo.

Fig 2.49 Half-foam Roll Split Squats (Varying Angles)

Single Leg Half-foam Roll Squats (Maintain Position)

This exercise will be a real challenge but may be useful in training for turns, and for those nightmarish moments when you find one ski up in the air and you have to regain balance on one leg while the other comes back to earth. Begin by performing a squat with one foot on the flat side of the half-foam roll and one foot on the floor, with the legs close to each other. Progress to having the foot that was on the floor raised and pointing downwards, so that you can balance yourself when necessary using the toes of that foot. Finally, perform the exercise entirely with the one foot that is on the foam roll, keeping the foam roll in the same position throughout.

Fig 2.50 Single Leg Half-foam Roll Squats (Maintain Position)

Single Arm Wood Chops with Single Leg Squats

This movement is a progression of the first Single Arm Wood Chops (*see* page 93). The only variation is that a squat is included on one leg. You can vary whether it is the leg on the same side as the exercising arm or the opposite leg. Both movements are useful and should be experimented with.

Alternate Single Leg Squats with Tuck on BOSU (Flat Side Up)

This movement is a slightly more dynamic progression of the single leg squats on the half-foam roll. Perform a Single Leg Squat with one foot slightly off centre on the BOSU, and then alternate

Fig 2.51 Wood Chops (Single Arm) with Single Leg Squats

to a Single Leg Squat on the other leg. The feet should be close enough to the centre of the BOSU that they touch when you alternate the squatting leg. In the bottom position of the Single Leg Squat, the body should be in a 'tuck' position, with the torso rounded forwards, before alternating legs.

Fig 2.52 Alternate Single Leg Squats with Tuck on BOSU (Flat Side Up)

Alternate Single Leg Squats with Tuck on BOSU
(Round Side Up)

This movement is similar to the previous exercise, but performed on the round side of the BOSU instead of the flat side. The movement is performed with one foot close to the centre of the BOSU, and the other held out behind the body. The foot on the BOSU should be kept in a relatively neutral position, by pressing into the side of the BOSU, through the inside of the foot. The opposite would be to allow the foot to turn inwards so that the whole foot is pressing into the BOSU, and the ankle is leaning away from the BOSU, which should be avoided. The non-squatting leg should be allowed to drift backwards during the movement to avoid the top of the BOSU, and as with the previous movement, the tuck should be performed on every repetition.

Fig 2.53 Alternate Single Leg Squats with Tuck on BOSU (Round Side Up)

Maintenance/Recovery Programme

- Front Squats (page 72)
- Forward Lunges (page 75)
- Step-ups (page 89)
- Side Step-ups (page 90)
- Russian Twists (page 73)
- Single Arm Wood Chops (page 93)

This programme acts as a break in the normal progression of the various phases. It can be used as required, with speed if you feel that you need to develop power, or just as a basic phase if you need to recover from the main programme. If you feel that your movement skills are fine, but you need to get back into the rhythm of general exercise before going through the more advanced exercises, then this could work well as a starting point.

Maintenance/Recovery Programme

Exercise	Sets	Reps	Rest
Front Squats	2–3	8	90
Lunges	2–3	8	90
Step-ups	2–3	8	90
Side Step-ups	2–3	8	90
Russian Twists	2–3	8	90
Wood Chops	2–3	8	90

Please refer to the photographs and explanations of these exercises in the earlier programmes.

Cooling Down

The purpose of the cool-down is to prepare the body to stop exercising. During the course of any of the programmes, your heart rate should have increased quite considerably, and it is not safe to simply stop exercising at the end of the last set. Instead, the heart rate needs to be gradually reduced so that it approaches a resting level (although actually achieving a resting level is highly unlikely). Failing to do this could lead to blood pooling in the legs, as the leg exercises require preferred blood flow, and the sudden stopping of exercise means that the blood is left in the legs for a short period of time. This can lead to faintness or dizziness, and if it happens then the remedy is to move the legs around to encourage the veins to shunt the blood back towards the heart.

The way the main body of the exercise programme is constructed is to begin with the most demanding exercises (perhaps following a couple of smaller exercises to ensure proper technique) and to finish on significantly less demanding exercises. A graph of the exerciser's heart rate would show a gradual increase through the warm-up and into the main body of the exercise session, and then after the last demanding exercise the heart rate would reduce towards the end of the main body of exercises. The cool-down should be a continuation of this to ensure it is safe to stop exercising. In some cases, the last exercise may be so easy that there is no need to perform any other specific 'cool-down' exercises.

When a deliberate cool-down is required, this can be completed on a piece of cardiovascular (CV) equipment, and this time any CV equipment that involves the legs should be sufficient (a specific exercise is not really required as at this point the goal is to get the body prepared for doing very little, rather than in preparation for exercises). If exercising at home, then a reversal of the warm-up is probably the most straightforward means of cooling down. Otherwise, walking around the home, running up and down some stairs, or anything else that comes to mind that begins with an elevated heart rate should suffice. The goal is to reduce the workload over time, so that after a few minutes the body is completely ready to finish exercise.

Stretching

Stretching is a rather complicated issue, and often either carried out ineffectively or disregarded altogether. There are many benefits to proper stretching, but it is important to understand why it is important, and its relevance to a skiing programme.

When a muscle is stretched, it returns to its normal length once the stretch is finished because it is elastic. This is an important point if the goal of stretching is to increase a muscle's length over the long term. Stretching has also been associated with reducing muscle soreness following exercise, through a sort of wringing effect on the muscle. When a muscle is trained, it is possible that it becomes tight in the days following the exercise session. This can alter the position of the associated joint, and eventually contribute to postural problems. Stretching can therefore be used as a means to help ensure that the joints are in their correct position, and that posture does not suffer over the long term.

If a muscle has become shorter than it is supposed to be, such as through the effects of exercise training, poor posture, injury, or fashion (such as wearing high heels), then it will be necessary to lengthen that muscle to ensure that it can work properly. For skiing, it is useful if the muscles at the back of the upper legs (hamstrings) are longer than would be required for normal activities of daily living. When bent forwards in a tuck position, the longer the hamstrings then the better the spine can be held in a more neutral position.

So, aside from general stretches associated with the exercise programme, it may also be necessary to stretch a particular muscle if there is a length discrepancy or insufficient range of motion, or specifically because it may be of benefit to some of the postures adopted when skiing. Assessing a length discrepancy or range of motion is something that could be done by a physiotherapist or appropriately qualified exercise professional. Self-testing is particularly difficult. Any queries on this issue could be checked with a physiotherapist or exercise professional.

The length of time that a stretch should be held depends on the intention of stretching. If stretching is just to compensate for the workout, then the stretches can be held for about 30 seconds. If the intention is to increase muscle length more permanently, then the stretches should be held for up to a few minutes each. As the feel of the stretch eases off, gently progress the stretch a little further.

Stretching in this manner should be repeated three times a week. There is also a lot of debate at the moment about the efficacy of static stretching, and for a number of different reasons, in particular with comparisons to movement-based flexibility. At the moment, a lack of scientific evidence for movement-based flexibility training means that there is nothing firm to include in the training literature.

Some guidelines for stretching individual muscles and parts of the body follow.

For a more detailed explanation of the anatomy and physiology of stretching, please see three related articles I have written for: www.ptonthenet.com

Chest Stretch

Stand with one hand pressing against a wall, with the arm extended out to the side. Slowly twist the body away from the arm until you feel a stretch in the shoulder.

Fig 2.54 Chest Stretch

Fig 2.55 Abdominals Stretch

Abdominals Stretch

Stand with one foot in front of the other and reach the arms back above and behind the body. If the pelvis is kept in the same position, or tilted downwards at the front, then the abdominals are stretched as the chest moves up.

Fig 2.56 Spinal Erectors Stretch

Spinal Erectors Stretch

Begin by getting into a tuck position as for skiing. Then wrap the arms around the underneath of the legs, just above the bent knees, and (keeping the lower body and arms fixed) push the back up towards the ceiling so that you stretch all the muscles that run down either side of the spine. Adjusting the angle of the hips, and how the spine is bent, can affect which areas of the spinal erectors are stretched. Experiment until you find the positions that elicit the best stretch.

Hip Flexors Stretch

Begin in a Split Squat position (*see* page 65) but bending forwards on the front leg, and extend the opposite arm up and across the body. If the pelvis is tilted downwards and the leg is stretched back, then the arm acts as a lever to pull the torso up and away from the hip, developing a stretch in the hip.

Quadriceps (Front of Thigh) Stretch

A standard stretch for the front of the thighs is to bend the knee so that the heel is close to the butt. The ankle can be supported by the arm on the same side, and the foot pulled further towards the butt, thereby increasing the stretch. The knees should be level at the beginning of the movement, and a progression to target a particular muscle in the quadriceps (as well as the hip flexors) can be achieved by allowing the knee on the stretched side to move slightly rearwards. The body should remain upright throughout.

Fig 2.57 Hip Flexors Stretch

Fig 2.58 Quadriceps (Front of Thigh) Stretch

Fig 2.59 Adductors Stretch

Adductors Stretch

This exercise is similar to the sideways lunge. Begin by stepping out to the side, keeping the other foot pointing forwards and that leg straight. The other leg (that moved out to the side) should be bent with the foot pointing out to the side, and the hands resting on that knee.

Hamstrings Stretch

Begin by taking a step forwards with one leg. Keep that leg straight and bend the other, pushing the hips back while keeping a neutral spine, until the knees are level with each other. The hands should be rested on the bent (back) leg. The stretch in the

Fig 2.60 Hamstrings Stretch

125

back of the straight leg can be accentuated by placing the front foot further forwards and sitting back more with the hips.

Fig 2.61 Glutes Stretch

Glutes Stretch

This stretch can be performed by standing upright on one leg and grasping the other around the knee and pulling it into the body. Different areas of the glute (butt) muscles can then be stretched by moving the knee slightly across the body, or changing the angle of the upper leg. The stretch can also be performed by resting the foot on a support and bending the other knee until a stretch is felt.

Gastrocnemius Stretch

The gastrocnemius is one of two muscles that make up the calves. To stretch this muscle you can perform a movement similar to a backward lunge. Step backwards while keeping the front (supporting) knee bent. Straighten the back leg and push the heel into the floor. Rest the hands on the front leg or push against a wall. The stretch can be accentuated by placing the back foot further out behind the body.

Fig 2.62 Gastrocnemius Stretch

Soleus Stretch

The soleus is the other muscle that makes up the calves. This can be stretched in a similar position to the stretch for the gastrocnemius but by bending the back knee to initiate the stretch.

Alternatively, use a block to brace the front foot against, and bend the front knee and lean forwards so that a stretch is initiated in the calf of the front leg.

Fig 2.63 Soleus Stretch

Cardiovascular Training

Cardiovascular (CV) fitness refers to how well your body works to get blood to where it is needed. The heart can become stronger and the smallest blood vessels can increase to allow greater delivery of blood to exercising areas. The greater someone's cardiovascular fitness, the more efficiently and comfortably they can perform cardiovascular exercise, such as running, cycling and even skiing. Cardiovascular exercise is essentially any exercise that aims to increase heart rate for a prolonged period. Although resistance training with weights increases heart rate, the regular rest periods mean it is not regarded as cardiovascular training in the same way as running or cycling.

Cardiovascular exercise also brings benefits when not exercising. Resting heart rate and blood pressure will eventually be reduced, metabolism will be increased, and the body will prioritise fat stores to be used for energy in greater ratios than carbohydrates. CV exercise also helps to relieve stress and improves mental wellbeing. Cholesterol levels will also be improved following a good cardiovascular programme.

When performing any exercise that causes heavy breathing and the associated discomfort, then improving cardiovascular fitness will delay the point at which that level of discomfort starts. If spending a day skiing, then the body is not only producing muscular effort and power for short periods of time, but is also expending greater amounts of energy throughout all the time spent on the slopes. This means that the better someone's cardiovascular fitness, the more energy they will have and the less tired they will become when skiing. This will have benefits in terms of overall enjoyment of skiing, and will also help to offset the fatigue associated with lapses in concentration and accidents.

Because we favour specific exercises, then aside from the warm-up exercises at the beginning of the main programme, it is quite difficult to find a truly specific cardiovascular exercise to replicate skiing. One solution could be to spend months by the slopes gradually increasing the workload and thereby finding the perfect solution to this problem. However, for those of us who live in warmer climes this is not possible, and although using artificial slopes is useful, it still will not challenge the body as much as an entire mountainside.

The best compromise if exercising at home is to spend a couple of sessions a week performing a prolonged warm-up over 20–30 minutes. This creates what is essentially a specific aerobics class (I can only wonder how long it will be before a new craze in Ski-Fit aerobics is born). If exercising in a gym, then some cross-trainers are very similar to skiing movements, although they are far from perfect. The next best is the treadmill, which at least permits exercise in an upright posture. Steppers, cycles and rowing machines are less specific and only for the general, rather than specific, benefits of cardiovascular exercise.

Following a progressive and thorough warm-up, the main cardiovascular exercise can last as long as you have available. As long as the session is slightly more difficult than the one that went before it, then benefits will be derived. The session should conclude with a thorough and gradual cool-down over a few minutes, or longer as required. It is necessary for the body to recover before performing cardiovascular exercise again, but two to three sessions per week of at least 20 minutes will be adequate to begin improving CV fitness and general health. Cardiovascular exercise predominantly utilises different muscle fibres to those used during heavy resistance work, so cardiovascular and resistance sessions can take place on consecutive days, or even on the same day. The trick is to start off gently, and exercise when you feel that the body is ready to do so.

nutrition

Some people would have us believe that we can eat what we want so long as we exercise sufficiently. Others regard exercise as something artificial, and believe that the key to a healthy mind and body is proper nutrition. Few and far between are the people who regard exercise and nutrition as equals. Exercise performance cannot be maintained or developed without a sufficient intake of all the required nutrients. Likewise, eating properly is of little consequence if there is no exercise-based stimulus to maintain a healthy body.

Having a good diet is not the preserve of the ultra-health-conscious and the dieter. Physical appearance, in terms of body weight, gives little indication of physical health. This is even more the case for people who exercise, for whom more nutrients are required for overall energy levels, repair and recovery following exercise, and maintaining the health of the body's cells and organs.

There are a few general dietary rules that most of us know but fail to apply effectively. There is such variety between individuals that it is not practical to dictate or advocate a particular dietary strategy for everyone. Instead, we have to try to find the foods that work best for us, and ensure we get all the nutrients we need.

There are two categories of nutrients:

1. The **macronutrients** are the carbohydrates, fats and proteins
2. The **micronutrients** are the vitamins and minerals

Today's diet fads tend to promote one type of macronutrient and criticise another. The arguments often contain a heavy bias that fails to take into account both sides of the story. In addition, because we are all so different, what might prove beneficial to some might be disastrous to others.

In the first instance, the best thing we can do is adopt a whole-food approach to nutrition. Whole foods are free from mechanical and chemical processing. Processed foods are generally higher in calories, salt and sugar, and have been broken down and heated up to the point where there is little real nutritional benefit to them. They might provide energy, but the body needs more than just energy. Our vitamins and minerals should come from good quality fruits and vegetables, eaten throughout the day. This means leaf and root vegetables, and a fruit intake that includes more than a solitary satsuma.

Carbohydrates can be found in rice, potatoes, fruits and vegetables. Proteins can be found in meats, fish, dairy products and eggs. Fats tend to be found in protein-rich foods in sufficient quantities. There are various different carbohydrates, proteins and fats, and there are none that should be avoided entirely. If there is a health problem related to diet, such as high blood pressure or cholesterol, then some foods may need to be avoided, but this is such an individual area that it is not possible to devote more space to it here. Instead, a dietician should investigate any dietary health problems.

In order to supply sufficient energy for exercise sessions and recovery afterwards, it is important to obtain enough carbohydrates from the diet. Proteins are also important for recovery. Fats are important for supplying the body with certain vitamins, and stored fat is preferentially used as energy as an adaptation to cardiovascular training. In short, we should eat plenty of everything and neglect nothing. Rather than giving specific quantities and ratios, which cannot be done here with any kind of accuracy for individuals, it is better simply to advise that people eat plenty of all the various foods that can be included in a whole-food diet.

While it is true that some people are healthier with a diet that prioritises a particular macronutrient, this sort of analysis should be sought through a dietician. In addition, it is important that people who want to lose weight prioritise reducing total calories rather than assuming that one particular type of macronutrient is to blame. The most accurate and yet basic advice, therefore, is to avoid processed foods in favour of whole foods, and then ensure a good variety of different foods so that everything the body needs can be obtained freely from the diet.

When exercising, it is best to eat carbohydrates before, and then a mix of carbohydrates and proteins soon after. The quantities and timing of these meals depends upon the individual, and there is a lot of trial and error to find out what works best. Fluid intake is also important. Even 1 per cent dehydration will have a negative effect on performance, so it is essential to make sure that water or an isotonic sports drink is available during exercise sessions. Our thirst response is actually quite ineffective. We only feel thirsty when we are already dehydrated, and then we can stop feeling thirsty by having a solitary, almost insignificant, mouthful of water. During exercise, the body can need approximately 250ml of fluid every 15 minutes.

On the Slopes

When away at a skiing resort it is likely that there will be some significant changes in the diet. This will most likely be due to the combination of food availability, and the fact that for most people skiing is a holiday, and when we are on holiday we like to treat ourselves to the sorts of food we would not eat much of otherwise. Because spending most of the day skiing requires a lot of energy, it is important to eat plenty of food, including more than we would expect when not exercising so much. So we therefore have permission to eat more, but it is still important to aim to eat a variety of whole foods, including fresh fruit and vegetables, to ensure that we have covered all our nutritional bases. The increased volume of exercise means that we have an increased requirement not just for energy, but for all the nutrients the body needs.

Having a good dinner will help to ensure that the body recovers effectively for the following day of skiing. The increased number of accidents following injury-free first days of skiing is often regarded as being related to fatigue. Proper nutrition will help reduce the chances of becoming fatigued on the slopes, and this approach will complement the need for proper exercise training.

Because energy, specifically carbohydrate, is reduced overnight, it is important to have a big breakfast in the morning. During the day it is also important to stop every few hours to top up on food. This could be integrated into a hot chocolate break in a piste-side chalet. Hot chocolate contains more energy than tea or coffee, before the addition of sugar, and the relative lack of caffeine is also preferential in the early part of the day. Because caffeine has a diuretic effect, taking some in during a break from exercise can increase dehydration. Sufficient intake of fluids is important to ensure hydration, so opportunities should be taken as often as possible, as dehydration can lead to fatigue and can even affect coordination.

Après-ski

Much as skiing holidays should prioritise skiing, there seems to have been an increase in the attitude that après-ski is what the holiday is all about. Certainly the social aspects of après-ski, and the opportunity to stock up on food and aid the body to recover, are good things. Alcohol, however, really should be taken only in moderation, if at all. The main reason for this is the safety of yourself and other skiers. Over the last few years we have come to accept that driving the morning after we have had a few drinks can still affect our coordination and reactions. This is therefore the same for skiing ability.

That is not to say that we should abstain from having a drink, but rather that we should be aware of how much we are drinking, and probably have a few fruit juices during the evening as well. Alcohol can deplete the body of some vitamins and minerals, so it is even more important to make sure we are eating plenty of good foods in the evening and for breakfast. Because alcohol is a diuretic, it also increases water loss, which can lead to dehydration. So, in summary, if we decide to have a drink, then we need to be aware of how much, and we need to take in plenty of other fluids and good foods to ensure that our skiing performance does not suffer as a result.

The Final Word

Unlike taking up running, cycling or fishing, skiing is an activity that places huge demands on the body through its sheer intensity. It is not the case that runners do not work hard, but a runner would be unlikely to do nothing for 50 weeks of the year, and then run for five or so hours a day, every day for two weeks. Yet this is precisely what many people do when they decide to take up skiing. More fortunate are those who can ski for most of the year, or the seasoned professionals who head off to the slopes and habitually condition themselves whenever they are not skiing. But most skiers are nowhere near this stage. Because of this, most offer themselves up to a huge risk of injury, or at least of tiring themselves out to the point of not enjoying themselves as much as they could.

Skiing is an exceptional activity because it is so demanding, and also because of the timelessness of the surroundings and the rush of the sport. The best way to ensure that you make the most of your precious time away is to train yourself for it and prepare accordingly. Proper preparation requires a multifaceted approach, encompassing physical conditioning, awareness of the mechanisms of injury, a good knowledge of the importance of proper nutrition, and then a good plan each day for attacking the slopes.

The rewards of this commitment to hard work centre on improving the body's fitness for skiing. Accomplishing this will leave you better able to enjoy the rigours of skiing, while promoting your ability to improve technical skills for an even greater physical and mental challenge on the slopes.

Notes

Notes

Notes

Notes

Notes

Notes